D1522010

Literature in Perspective

General Editor: Kenneth Grose

The Metaphysical Poets

Literature in Perspective

The Metaphysical Poets

Jim Hunter

Evans Brothers Limited London

Published by Evans Brothers Limited
Montague House, Russell Square, London W.C.1

© Jim Hunter 1965

First published 1965
Third reprint 1972

Set in 11 on 12 point Fournier and printed in Great Britain by
C. Tinling & Co. Ltd, London and Prescot

ISBN 0 237 44568 9 cased   PR 2776

ISBN 0 237 44462 3 limp

Literature in Perspective

Of recent years, the ordinary man who reads for pleasure has been gradually excluded from that great debate in which every intelligent reader of the classics takes part. There are two reasons for this: first, so much criticism floods from the world's presses that no one but a scholar living entirely among books can hope to read it all; and second, the critics and analysts, mostly academics, use a language that only their fellows in the same discipline can understand.

Consequently criticism, which should be as 'inevitable as breathing'—an activity for which we are all qualified—has become the private field of a few warring factions who shout their unintelligible battle cries to each other but make little communication to the common man.

Literature in Perspective aims at giving a straightforward account of literature and of writers—straightforward both in content and in language. Critical jargon is as far as possible avoided; any terms that must be used are explained simply; and the constant preoccupation of the authors of the Series is to be lucid.

It is our hope that each book will be easily understood, that it will adequately describe its subject without pretentiousness so that the intelligent reader who wants to know about Donne or Keats or Shakespeare will find enough in it to bring him up to date on critical estimates.

Even those who are well read, we believe, can benefit from a lucid exposition of what they may have taken for granted, and perhaps—dare it be said?—not fully understood.

K. H. G.

5

The Metaphysical Poets

This book is about the so-called Metaphysical poets of the seventeenth century, confining itself almost entirely to those it sees as 'important': Donne, Herbert, Crashaw, Vaughan and Marvell.

The book does not lay claim to much, if any, original thought: the bibliography at the back should be taken also as a list of those to whom it is indebted. Nor does it attempt to offer expert elucidations of notoriously difficult poems. Such analysis and criticism as will be found here is always related to the fundamental purpose of the book, which is to give an *initial* understanding of and feeling for the poetry. The book is a beginning only, and should lead to further reading.

Parts of the book are deliberately elementary. They are fundamental to an understanding of what comes later, which is concerned with philosophical concepts of considerable complexity. Since, in studies of this kind, we so often tend to think we know or understand what we are actually hazy about, it seems essential to me to define the groundwork in simple terms. Without it, we can only flounder in increasing difficulties.

The book opens, not with the Metaphysical poets themselves, but by describing the times in which they lived. It tries to bridge some of the gaps in customs and ideas between then and now. It closes with a short history of critical judgements on the Metaphysicals through the centuries. This is a strange story, which it might be as well to glance at—unless you are well informed on the subject—before reading the rest.

In this book, 'Metaphysical' with a capital M means: 'of the particular literary type exemplified by Donne and his followers'.

Where the word is used in its ordinary philosophical sense, it is printed with a small m. The difference between the two meanings is discussed at the beginning of Chapter 2.

I have frequently borrowed ideas and observations from critical books on the Metaphysicals, without making any reference to the source (unless, of course, it is quoted directly). This is contrary to academic practice, but seems to me to be, for readers who are not professional scholars, a good idea. In any case, these debts, considerable as they are, are really less than those which I owe to friends who have advised me: in particular, to Kenneth Grose of Bradford Grammar School, the editor of the Series, and to Dr. A. H. Gomme of the University of Keele.

J. H.

Contents

The Author

Jim Hunter, M.A., is Senior English Master at Bristol Grammar School. He has published four novels, two anthologies of modern fiction, and another volume in this series, on *Gerard Manley Hopkins*.

Acknowledgements

The portrait of John Donne is reproduced by kind permission of the Marquess of Lothian, and the portrait of Andrew Marvell is reproduced by permission of the National Portrait Gallery. The photograph of Sir William Cordell's monument is by Neals, Photographers, Norwich, and the portrait of Richard, Earl of Dorset, is reproduced by permission of the Victoria and Albert Museum, Crown Copyright.

I

Background

John Donne was born in 1572; Henry Vaughan died in 1695, but seems to have written little poetry after 1655. The best Metaphysical poetry was probably written between about 1595 and 1660. These were eventful years during which England survived considerable changes; they pass from the exciting but unsettled reign of Elizabeth I through James I to Charles I, the Civil War, and finally the Restoration. To understand Metaphysical poetry one does not need detailed knowledge of the history of the period; but some awareness of the way people thought at the time is a big help.

It was a time of unrest, as well as of glory. The richest period of our literature, and one of the richest of our music, it was nevertheless a dangerous time. Even if one did not live in constant fear of imprisonment or execution because of what one believed or did not believe, one might be even more profoundly disturbed, inwardly, by the way so many of society's foundations seemed threatened. The nature of kingship, of divinity, and of authority in general; the nature of individual man, and his right to govern himself; these questions were the gripping issues of the age, and were enough to rouse men to war and personal sacrifice.

The historian, standing back and making rather abstract generalisations, can suggest that it was the Renaissance, and its aftermath, which provoked much of this unrest. An account of the Renaissance lies, obviously, outside the scope of this book; it was the first of the two great European artistic and philosophical developments of thought which have occurred since medieval times, the other being Romanticism. The two movements had much in common: both spoke optimistically of the potential of individual man, and favoured energetic exploration in the arts; and both brought in their wake scepticism and unrest, when the first thrill had passed.

Today, when we can calmly say that we are sure of very little, and when, in particular, the dictates of a religion or a monarch no longer make us tremble, Donne's age may seem to have very confident and even rigid beliefs. But by comparison with medieval times, and even with the early years of Renaissance thought, it was revolutionary, without quite seeming to know where it was going (a common characteristic of revolutionary feeling).

All of us know something of the voyages of plunder and exploration in the days of Elizabeth. They make good adventure stories, and they must have been exciting to people of the time: the jewels and precious minerals, the destruction of the Spanish Armada, the introduction of curiosities which were to become addictions (the tobacco leaf and the potato), and, most of all, the revelations of whole areas of the world which were unknown. The world itself, only recently proved to be round, was a new concept to be grasped; and before long Galileo was establishing that the world was not the centre of things, but only one in a group of subordinates, moving round the sun.

All this was exciting, but frightening, too. Centuries of colonial rivalry between European countries were beginning, and England's clashes with Spain were only one indication of what might lie ahead. When the size of the world was calculated, you realised how little of it was known at all; when the very position of the world in the heavens was revised, many other once-accepted beliefs were shaken. Astronomy, or its ancestor astrology, has always lain close to religious belief in men's minds.

Throughout the plays of Marlowe and Shakespeare, and in the poetry of the Metaphysicals, there are restless references to these fears, these uncertainties. On subjects such as astrology, alchemy, witchcraft, fairies, and even divinity, the writers hover between belief and disbelief; often they use the protective device of irony, to avoid committing themselves. But above all they are excited—and frightened—by man as individual, the free-ranging figure who might not be bound at all—who could be quite sure?—by the gods or God, or by morality. (Some readers will know *The Prince*, by Niccolo Machiavelli, a ruthlessly honest book about organised human societies, which, however horrified Elizabethans pretended to be by it, they knew secretly was at least partly true.)

The exaltation of man, in ways medieval thinkers would have thought to be those of Lucifer, into possibilities of unlimited greatness—this was the work of the Renaissance in sixteenth-century Europe; and it produced immense artistic successes, works of a far grander conception than had been seen since classical times. Much fine Renaissance art is dedicated directly to God; but much is also entirely secular, dedicated to man. Shakespeare's plays—the richest and most ambitious art of the age—are a vivid example. The arrogance of Marlowe's Tamburlaine, or of Donne's love-lyrics—however much they are explained as being 'dramatic'—is something entirely new, and we still respond to the sense of mastery with discovery which we find there.

But when this freedom and ambition were linked, as they were in late Elizabethan and Jacobean England, to the questioning of so many established beliefs, they could become something desperate and pessimistic. One feels sometimes, in Jacobean drama or in Donne, that perhaps man really is on his own, in which case he is dwarfed by the universe, and that morality and divinity are illusions. Those who know *King Lear* or *Hamlet* will be familiar with the feeling.

These are abstract matters, and because they are clearer to a historian than they were to men of the time, there is a danger that we over-estimate their importance. Perhaps only a particularly sensitive and wide-ranging mind would then have been aware of such disturbances, and then, only when an artist such as Shakespeare or Donne, referred to them obliquely, in his art.

But there were very concrete disturbances in Europe. As always, wars were being fought; and they were predominantly religious. In Britain, the war was delayed until 1640, but then it was a Civil War, and it had been brewing some while.

Although the years of most unrest—1640-60—come at the end of our period, they were only the climax of many decades of anxiety. In 1600 England was governed by the monarch, with the assistance of Parliament. (Today, of course, whatever foreigners believe, she is governed entirely by Parliament.) Ultimately the Parliament was bound to fall out with the monarch. Even in 1600 there was friction and division; Elizabeth's favour could vary, there were bitter rivalries between factions, and there was much anxiety about the successor to the queen, who was unmarried and childless. The subsequent reign of the 'foreigner' James, who tried to assert authority at points where it would have been wiser to be more tentative, helped to make it conceivable that, fifteen years after his death, Parliament and half the country should turn against his son.

Charles I's reign saw a clearer aligning of religious with political factions: Charles's wife, Henrietta Maria, was a foreigner and a Roman Catholic; there were persistent rumours of a Popish plot to subordinate England again to Roman authority; and the Puritans and Parliamentarians began to pool their grievances, where they were not already united. As regards the monarchy, the great questions were: how absolute is the king's authority, or his wisdom? Is he divinely appointed? Should he be allowed to appropriate public money more or less as he chooses? May he impose his religious belief upon the land?

To a considerable extent, in the seventeenth century, politics and religion were the same thing.

Men had always been deeply religious, in so far that they credited the words of priests and were filled with genuine fear of heavenly power. What was rather new, in the time of Shakespeare and Donne, was the increasing feeling among thinking men that one might possibly not have been born into the true religion—that it was up to oneself to think it out. There was even a small current of atheism moving, though to admit sympathies with it was very dangerous. A great many men, from the Renaissance onwards, were 'modern' in feeling strong religious instinct without being sure which, if any, Church had the truth. From the evidence of his plays, Shakespeare seems to have been such a man. Other writers of the period are instanced below to show the way an intelligent man might fluctuate.

Christopher Marlowe is said to have talked atheism. His plays also often seem to question established authority—yet his most moving passage is the death of Faustus, which seems to carry firm Christian conviction. Ben Jonson, the son of a Protestant minister, was for twelve years in the middle of his life a Roman Catholic, then went back to the English Church. John Donne, born a Roman Catholic, became a devout Anglican. Richard Crashaw, son of a Puritan, became a High Church Anglican at Cambridge, and finally went abroad and became a Roman Catholic. Henry Vaughan does not seem to have flirted with another religion, but is worth mentioning as an example of a man powerfully converted from a frivolous to a religious life. Finally, Andrew Marvell, another clergyman's son, was born a Protestant, was a Catholic for a short time in his youth, became a close friend of the Puritans Cromwell and Milton, yet was able to hold his parliamentary seat for twenty years after the Restoration!

Herbert and Milton, the only great poets of the period not mentioned above, were intensely religious poets; all the above writers can be said to have written on religion, most of them extensively. 'Nearly half the books' published in England between 1600 and 1640, it has been suggested, were on religious topics. Religion was the first interest in the hearts of a great number, perhaps a majority, of Englishmen.

All this is background. The reader of the Metaphysical poets will find few references to contemporary affairs; if we had only the poems, and no histories, it is unlikely that we should know of the Civil War. Yet fundamentally the crises and preoccupations outlined above are present in the poems. The work of Donne and Marvell, with its nervous ironic edge—Donne's rougher than Marvell's—is in the key of the most sensitive minds of their age. And if Herbert and Vaughan are seen as different, still there is in both poets the continual mention of religious difficulty. Both write from the humility of men seeking, and so are marvellously free of the complacency or unthinking acceptance which often appears in medieval or eighteenth-century religious poets. Crashaw is another matter again; those particularly interested in Crashaw should read Odette de Mourgues' fine essay, in the Pelican *Donne to Marvell*, on the baroque as an outcome of the tensions existing in European thought of his time.

THE POET IN SOCIETY

Poetry today often seems to feel it needs an apologia. In this 'democratic' century, the fact that poetry appeals to only a minority makes it dubious in some people's eyes, even some of those who like poetry themselves. The very word suggests to many laymen something 'affected' or 'precious'.

Things were not at all like this in Elizabethan or seventeenth-century England. Certainly, as in all ages, there were some 'precious' and flowery poets; and they were cheerfully mocked. (One of the achievements of Metaphysical poetry, as Chapter 4 says, was to write simply, clearing away the hackneyed prettinesses of ordinary Elizabethan verse.) Nevertheless, most of the sixteenth- and seventeenth-century poets known today were men in the centre of worldly society: business men, scientists, soldiers, sailors and politicians. Learning to write poetry had been a part of their essential education for the civilised life; and an enormous amount of poetry was written under no pressure of inspiration or what we today would call 'sincere' feeling, but simply because it was one of the things a gentleman might do, to prove himself the more gentleman.

All the major Metaphysicals may be called gentleman-poets: Donne accepted patronage, but moved in noble circles, was a Member of Parliament (as were Herbert and Marvell also), and had hopes of a court position. And gentleman-poets distinguished themselves in many ways apart from their poetry. Their biographies are full of battles, imprisonments, knighthoods, blood-and-thunder (Marlowe was killed in a political brawl, Fulke Greville was murdered, Ben Jonson killed a colleague,

Sir Walter Ralegh and Robert Southwell were executed) and, above all, activity in the cause of religion. Poetry was to many only a sideline; there was certainly no risk of their becoming literary recluses.

It might seem, then, that poetry was unimportant to them—simply a social grace like dancing or card-playing. On the contrary: what strikes us the more from reading the biographies and the poetry side by side is that these men should have made time to write, with such care, and with such intense feeling. Far from being of minor importance, poetry was to the best of these men their ultimate and finest form of expression, to which they would turn in moments of particular urgency. The most vivid example of this is Sir Walter Ralegh's *The Passionate Man's Pilgrimage* (a poem, incidentally, which has many of the characteristics described in Chapter 2 as Metaphysical). This was written (we are almost certain) during a period when the writer was under sentence of death, not knowing when he might be led from prison to the execution-block. The following lines exemplify several qualities of the gentleman-poet; in particular, they are deepened by something which will be mentioned and praised several times in this book, the humility of a sense of humour (the fourth line here):

> And this is my eternal plea,
> To him that made Heaven, Earth, and Sea:
> Seeing my flesh must die so soon,
> And want a head to dine next noon,
> Just at the stroke when my veins start and spread
> Set on my soul an everlasting head . . .

The following notes may sum up the social position of a poet, including those who were not born noblemen and who wrote for money:

1. To a good poet no level of society was necessarily barred. Civilised society read much poetry, with enthusiasm and with some discrimination.

2. Publication was haphazard; we cannot be sure that it was always with the author's consent; and in any case he would not

be paid large sums. The money, as Shakespeare and Jonson showed, lay in the theatre, in plays commissioned by a company of players. Poems were most frequently circulated in manuscript copies; and those poets without a private income would hope first for a nobleman's patronage rather than for *earnings* from writing. The Grub Street of Alexander Pope's England had yet to develop.

3. In spite of (2) there is much evidence that a poet's work, if striking, would rapidly become well known, or talked of; and poets would (as they do today) read each other's work avidly, looking for new developments or fashions.

4. What is more, most of the important London poets would know one another. Critics sometimes show surprise that Shakespeare was a friend of Jonson, and Jonson of Donne, and Donne of Herbert; and today for the four greatest poets of an age to be so linked would be remarkable—but not impossible. In 1600, however, London—though by far the largest English city—was only about as big as present-day Bradford or Nottingham: about three hundred thousand people, of whom only a small minority could read and write. It is hardly surprising that there was in London at that time an intimacy of connection between poet and poet, and between the literary circle and the court circle, hard for us to imagine.

TRADITIONS IN POETRY

A. Form

The versatility of Donne's age is stressed several times in this book; and it is shown in poetry as much as elsewhere. Song, sonnet, long philosophical meditation, epic, satire, and of course the serious stanzaic poem for which we have never found a really good name ('lyric' being rather misleading): all these were written in Donne's age, and he himself wrote some of all kinds except the epic. He and the other Metaphysicals are, however, best known for their shorter poems, which we shall concentrate on in this book.

Probably the shorter poems even then were the most popular; they would certainly reach the widest audience. Donne used the forms used by other Elizabethan poets, and did some new things with them. Carew, in his obituary poem on Donne, says that he gave poetry a new freshness and excellence; but this was done not by the invention of new forms, but by the unexpected and personal handling of the accepted ones. Chapters 3, 4 and 5 naturally have much to say about this.

The most popular short forms were the song, the 'lyric' poem deriving directly from song, and the sonnet. In the later Metaphysical poets, because of the fashion of the age, the sonnet drops completely out of use, while a form rare in Elizabethan times, the eight-syllable (tetrameter) couplet, becomes very frequent.

1. *The Song:* Much of the richness of Elizabethan music manifests itself in song: fine words, written by leading poets of the day, finely set. A number—particularly those by Shakespeare, written for the theatre—are still widely known today. The song-form demands of the writer regularity of stanza (though the stanza may and often does have its own unusual shape), directness and clarity of statement, avoiding complex sentence-structures, and a minimum of enjambement (running over into the next line). Very few Metaphysical poems are in the song-form, because of the complexity of their statements; but the poems of Donne, at least, contain many examples of brisk and lilting stanza-form.

2. *The Lyric Poem in Stanzas:* This form, particularly where it approached song, was made popular, in their different ways, by Donne and Jonson, both of whom had many followers. Although it allowed for intricacy of stanza, it represented a loosening and liberation from the more sober forms of the sixteenth century, particularly in its use of light, short lines. Neatness and dexterity of rhythm were approved qualities, and these principles undoubtedly produced such mid-century technical experts as Suckling, Lovelace, Herrick and Waller.

3. *The Sonnet:* The sonnet was immensely popular with the more serious-minded Elizabethan poets, stimulated by Continental fashion. Both the 'Shakespearean' (*ababcdcdefef.gg*) and the 'Petrarchan' (*abbaabba.cdecde*) forms, with variants, were used; and sonnets were written in often long sequences, addressed

to a beloved or a patron. The best-known today, deservedly, are those of Shakespeare; but to appreciate Donne's poetry one needs to know that most Elizabethan sonneteers showed far less imagination or variety than Shakespeare, and were content to repeat the same images and ideas many times. The form was extremely stylised and artificial; one could almost always predict, after one quatrain (four lines) what a poet was going to say, and very often what image he was going to use. Donne's love-poetry is to some extent a fiery reaction against all this; and when he does return to the sonnet, for dignity, in his Holy Sonnets, he achieves a directness, simplicity, and drama which revolutionise the form.

B. *The First Person*

In the vast majority of Elizabethan poems the first person is used. This was a Renaissance characteristic, though naturally it had appeared occasionally earlier (e.g. in medieval religious lyrics). After the Restoration the attentions of literature turned, at least superficially, outwards again, towards society, and the leading poets of the next hundred years—Dryden, Pope, Johnson, Goldsmith, Gray—use 'I' comparatively little (notice how Gray avoids it in that very personal poem *Elegy in a Country Churchyard*). With Romanticism the individual was really liberated and the first person became the *normal* method of communication. But the two 'I's are very different, the Renaissance and the Romantic; and in this fact lies a great danger for a modern reader.

Today we all realise that when a pop singer sings—however passionately—'I love you', that is a convention: it is part of the song, part of the act, and the fact that it is 'insincere' doesn't matter at all. But when a modern poet uses 'I', we usually tend to take that as a genuine personal statement, as, usually, it is meant to be. Now, since Elizabethan lyric poetry was still closely linked to song, and since poetry itself was always known to be a convention, an Elizabethan 'I' was ambiguous. It might be as 'sincere' as the modern poet's 'I', or it might be as 'insincere' as that of the pop singer. The Elizabethan poet had it, as we say, both ways; and he and his audience knew it.

Donne's *Songs and Sonets* (the word 'sonet' meaning here just another kind of songlike poem) and some of Marvell's poetry offer this difficulty for us today. Even the apparently confessional poems of Herbert and Vaughan are not certain to be 'true'. Yet if we can forget our modern expectations, and accept the strange mixture of conventional and heartfelt statements as the original readers did, we can share their special appreciation of it.

C. Wit

We shall find this uncertainty about the 'sincerity' of a poet easier to understand if we are aware of the emphasis placed at the time upon Wit. This is a concept anyone wanting really to understand poetry written between, say, 1550 and 1750 must grasp.

Forget the modern, very limited meaning of the word. Think instead of German *wissen*—to know, and of the English *wise* and *wisdom* which are cognate with it. 'Wist ye not' in the Bible means 'don't you know'; and today we still speak of doing something 'wittingly' or 'unwittingly'.

Wit, then, meant *awareness*; and by a rapid extension it also meant cleverness, intelligence, the fine application of learning. In Elizabeth's time it was mainly applied to a man's conversation and writing. For poets it was the word used simply where we would say 'imagination' or 'skill'; if you were not 'witty' you were doing the thing clumsily.

It is not merely a difference of usage. If *wit* meant something like 'good writing' to an Elizabethan, we must be sure we understand what an Elizabethan took 'good writing' to be.

To be a 'witty' writer, you had to have a brain, and show it. To some extent you were a showman, and you earned the highest praise if, in doing the most daring things, you did them with an appearance of nonchalance. Emotion, sensitivity, piety were appreciated; but to make such material into poetry you had to organise and arrange it, so that it was a real construction, and so that it was civilised and urbane (this was where the control of a slight irony or sense of humour was so valuable). The feeling of a poem might be fundamentally sad; but to make a good poem of it you had to do something *with* that sadness, to show skill, ingenuity and control.

The result was that the most spontaneous cries from the heart —reaching almost to the *un*conscious—which we find in the best nineteenth-century poetry, were lacking; but so also were clumsiness, self-pity and mushy emotion. In the 'toughening-up' of poetic taste which occurred between 1910 and 1930, the urbane and elegant control of passion, which is found in sixteenth- and seventeenth-century poetry, came right back into favour, and the demands of Wit were appreciated once more. Listen, if you can, to the record of T. S. Eliot reading his own *Love-Song of J. Alfred Prufrock*; or, at least, read the poem.

You could be witty when your heart was involved, or where it was not. There was no question of 'sincere' feeling being essential to a poem, if the imagined feeling was well created. Perhaps a skilful feigning of emotion was more admired, in some circles, than an actual personal statement; certainly one of the most respected ways of writing a poem was to take an extremely well-known situation—such as The Rejected Lover, or The Lover Persuading His Lady (Let us love now, for tomorrow we die; known as the *Carpe Diem* theme)—and try to treat it freshly. In love-poetry Donne and Marvell frequently do this; in religious poetry Herbert and Vaughan do much the same, for example with the theme of rebellion. The most brilliant example of this in Metaphysical poetry (and, perhaps, in English) is Marvell's *To His Coy Mistress*—a *Carpe Diem* poem. This was probably not written to any particular girl at any particular time: it is very much within a 'witty' convention; but it is one of the most admired poems in our language.

D. Courtly Love

This in turn leads us to a note upon the conventions of love-poetry at the time. If you remember what has been said about Wit and 'sincerity', you will guess that you must not regard the love-poetry of Donne and others as strictly autobiographical. It may nevertheless still strike you as slightly shocking, in its apparently complete indifference to marriage or Christian morality. Donne and Marvell, you might think, must have been unpleasant hypocrites to write such love-poems in addition to religious poetry.

The short answer is, again, that it was convention. Probably it bore no closer relationship to the way people actually behaved than an evening's television programmes bear to our lives today. Some psychologists tell us that gangster-films are a safety-valve for release of our aggressive instincts; perhaps the gay liberty of Elizabethan amorous poetry acted similarly on the desires of love.

More particularly: there was still in Elizabethan times something of the medieval tradition of Courtly Love. This was a pose, a fashion, an attitude towards love which belonged to literature rather than to life: according to it, the really exciting love affairs were conducted outside marriage. They were either Platonic or, at least, noble and of lofty formality; the tradition is not to be confused with the cuckold tradition in low comedy or the mistress tradition in modern France. Again, it is probable that the literature of Courtly Love tells us very little about how people actually behaved. For one thing, most people really prefer the stability of marriage to the uneasiness of a glamorous tangle; and secondly, to conduct an affair according to the rules of Courtly Love must really have been rather a strain (Chaucer's *Knight's Tale* seems to be making this point). Formality and passion might go together in poetry, but not easily in life.

Clearly Donne's fierce love-poems are not in the formal tone of Courtly Love. But it may be worth our remembering that the leading medieval tradition of love-poetry assumed that (*within its artificial framework*) mistresses were the thing. Discrepancy between the poet's life and his poetry was entirely normal; and this still held true in Donne's day. The reader of many Victorian writers who sing loud and long the praises of lily-like purity might well take into consideration the sometimes sordid lives those writers actually led; certainly the reader of Donne should know that these versatile and sometimes licentious poems may well have little or no foundation in Donne's personal life. (The subject is discussed in Chapter 6.)

This chapter must not be allowed to daunt you. It is quite possible to read and enjoy Metaphysical poetry without having *any* background knowledge; its subjects are timeless and even its expression comparatively free from extinct references.

Conversely, for someone seeking a really firm knowledge of the Metaphysicals and their age, this chapter is only a beginning. Read the relevant sections of a History of England or similar authority; the general essays in the Pelican Guide (*Donne to Marvell*) are valuable also. Sample, if you are interested, the music and art of the period. Finally, remember that Donne's England, if not that of the later Metaphysicals, was also Shakespeare's England, upon which there are several good books. A reading of Shakespeare himself, or of an anthology of Elizabethan poetry, would also be of much value.

2

Characteristics of Metaphysical Poetry

The phrase 'Metaphysical poetry' is used in this book without quotation marks or apology, even though it has long been felt to be less than satisfactory. It grew, as is said in Chapter 9, from the disparaging remarks of some Restoration or eighteenth-century critics (see pages 151–2). But it has so long been accepted as an identifying name for the poets discussed in this book that a change now would be fussy and confusing; and in fact most literary terms of this kind are more or less inaccurate.

Strictly, 'metaphysical' means 'concerned with the fundamental problems of the nature of the universe, and man's place or function in life'. 'Philosophical' might be the modern word. This description might really be applied to all great poetry; but at least we can feel that it is not *inappropriately* applied to Donne and his successors, for in their poetry, which is remarkable for its intellectual energy, metaphysical and religious concerns do appear often, not only in subject but also in metaphor.

Here are some quotations from well-known Metaphysical poems, in which a metaphysical quality may be seen:

> We then, who are this new soul, know
>   Of what we are composed, and made,
> For the Atomies, of which we grow,
>   Are souls, whom no change can invade. . . .

THE ECSTASY, Donne

> And therefore her Decrees of Steel
> Us as the distant Poles have placed,

(Though Love's whole world on us doth wheel)
Not by themselves to be embraced.

THE DEFINITION OF LOVE, Marvell

I saw Eternity the other night. . . .

THE WORLD, Vaughan

Meanwhile the Mind, from pleasure less,
Withdraws into its happiness:
The Mind, that Ocean where each kind
Does straight its own resemblance find;
Yet it creates, transcending these,
Far other Worlds, and other Seas;
Annihilating all that's made
To a green Thought in a green Shade.

THE GARDEN, Marvell

Much Metaphysical poetry is religious, and so might be expected to be about first and last things, eternity, the soul, and the mind. But three of the above examples are not from what we would normally call religious poems. The love-poems of Donne, Marvell and their minor associates are as full of 'metaphysical' metaphor and exploration as the religious poems of Herbert, Vaughan, and Crashaw.

Probably, as Chapter 1 suggested, the time helped to produce these preoccupations. The new discoveries of voyagers, the new theories of scientists, theologians and politicians—all made a shake-up in the inquiring mind, and set its sights upon the nature of the universe, the validity of ideas of Heaven and Hell, the truth even of a man's own emotions. The poet was expected to be a man of wit (see pages 21-2), displaying not only his sensitivity but also his knowledge and cleverness; and the frequency of references in Metaphysical poetry to religious debate, astrology, alchemy, sea-discovery and philosophy illustrates the intellectual excitement of the age. So, of course, do the plays of William Shakespeare.

There is, then, some justification for the use of the adjective 'metaphysical' to describe the work of these poets. But the clearest distinguishing feature of Metaphysical poetry is the repeated combination of these 'metaphysical' elements with that particular type of metaphor called a *conceit*, which will be described in a moment.

BRAINWORK IN POETRY

Sixteenth-century verse is mostly that of men who had received a considerable education. It is always the product of intellectual effort as much as of emotion; the two must combine. Neither strong feeling nor brainwork would on its own make good poetry; just as the two should be balanced in a man, so the reader expected to respond to both in poetry—and to find them balanced.

A great deal has been written about this (and in particular, homage is always paid to T. S. Eliot's essay on the Metaphysical poets, in which he says that more recently the strong feeling and the brainwork have become separated in poetry, to our loss). It is a tricky matter for us, and a reader should make a special effort to understand—and appreciate—the conception of poetry held by an Elizabethan or Jacobean.

Later in this chapter it will be said that the extremes of emotion are almost always moderated, or controlled, in the Metaphysicals, by a sense of humour. This is a sign that the poet is still thinking; his critical intelligence is always at work, keeping a sense of proportion, and struggling to express *clearly* (not merely powerfully) what he feels. Coleridge said that in Shakespeare's poetry 'the creative power and the intellectual energy wrestle as in a war dance'; and this could just as well be applied to the Metaphysicals.

We may think we understand and agree with this, and yet not realise how different are our own preconceptions. This is where we may be puzzled by some aspects of Metaphysical poetry.

In the last hundred and fifty years we have been given much art which, for all its skill, springs mainly from a bursting emotional excitement and is directed mainly at the emotions of its audience. Two early examples of this which most readers will know are Shelley's *Ode to the West Wind* and Beethoven's Fifth Symphony. Both these works are written within traditional disciplines, but nearly burst their bounds in the untempered violence of their emotion; and later writers following them carried this change much further. Today the caricature-Romantic image which resulted from that change is the popular idea of the artist: a man of sudden extravagant Inspiration, dashing off masterpieces in half-hours between fits of insanity. Perhaps there was already something of this in Donne's day; in *A Midsummer Night's Dream* Shakespeare links 'the lunatic, the lover, and the poet'; and the emotional exaggeration which threatened that the poet would waste away and die as a result of a mistress's unkindness was a favourite of Elizabethan poets (and of Donne). But in practice in the sixteenth and seventeenth centuries a poem which did not require brainwork would not be admired; and conversely, to write a poem not because pressing emotion demanded it but as a technical exercise for one's 'wit' was a completely acceptable possibility—today it is thought to be vaguely fraudulent!

The sonnet-sequences which Elizabethan poets sent to their lovers or patrons exemplify this last fact. A constant overflowing of passion in fifty or a hundred poems (in a form as technically difficult as the sonnet) would be impossible. The effort and skill needed to produce the sonnets constituted much of the homage which a sonnet-sequence was meant to offer. This must be remembered frequently when one is reading the Metaphysicals; there are poems written for special occasions, love-poems written to provoke, to experiment with an unusual emotional tone, or to attempt a fresh treatment of a hackneyed idea, and sequences of religious poetry (in particular Herbert's *The Temple*) contrived and manufactured as an offering in worship. When we see how superb many of these poems are we are forced to modify the Romantic notion of immediate inspiration.

THE CONCEIT

Craftsmanship and cleverness, then, were things to be proud of, if well used. Much Elizabethan poetry is consequently ostentatiously skilful. The conjuror shows as he goes how the trick is done, and may even pass comments, aside, upon his craft (see Shakespeare's Sonnets 103 and 108, where he turns his *lack* of inspiration into a compliment to his subject). The *conceit* is a metaphor or simile intellectually contrived and drawn out in this ostentatious way. It is a particularly artificial means of comparison, and is given great attention for itself, not merely for the resemblance it is theoretically pointing. Shakespeare's earlier plays, being the best-known Elizabethan writing, offer examples. This is one of Romeo's most famous speeches, from *Romeo and Juliet*:

> But soft! what light through yonder window breaks?
> It is the east, and Juliet is the sun.
> Arise, fair sun, and kill the envious moon
> Who is already sick and pale with grief
> That thou, her maid, art far more fair than she . . .
> Two of the fairest stars in all the heaven,
> Having some business, do entreat her eyes
> To twinkle in their spheres till they return.
> What if her eyes were there, they in her head?
> The brightness of her cheek would shame those stars,
> As daylight doth a lamp; her eyes in heaven
> Would through the airy region stream so bright
> That birds would sing and think it were not night.

2, 2, 2-22

This is not in any way realistic writing, nor is it the outpouring of violent passion. It is a *representation* of passion within a highly formal convention, and it is the poet showing off how beautifully he can work within this convention. Notice, particularly, how the 'sun' metaphor is taken up again after being dropped momentarily, and how the poet works as much as he can out of it. Usually this is a characteristic of the conceit—a full and ingenious development which, to modern tastes, may seem to go a bit far.

Critics distinguish between a conceit and an ordinary poetic metaphor, and, often, between a Metaphysical conceit and any other kind. These distinctions worry many students, some of whom avoid the whole issue, while others pretend they understand when they really don't. The following notes may help.

In the more orthodox uses of poetic metaphor, A is being described, and is referred to temporarily in terms of B, because

29

in one respect, though perhaps in no other, they are similar. The poet's aim is to describe A, and B is only mentioned to illuminate A (or perhaps to bring in certain emotional suggestions). The following is, in textbook terms, a simile not a metaphor, but it illustrates the orthodox poetic image:

My love is like a red, red rose.

Here, if we think momentarily of rose-gardens, of smooth fine petals, of powerful fragrance (as is intended), nevertheless our attention returns almost immediately to the girl; the work of the image is to transfer the rose's attributes to her. And often the process is almost sub-conscious, we do not pause to work out the metaphor at all; the various Bs are only glanced at for their emotional associations. This is a complex example:

And all our yesterdays have lighted fools
The way to dusty death. Out, out, brief candle!
Life's but a walking shadow, a poor player
That struts and frets his hour upon the stage
And then is heard no more . . .

MACBETH, 5, 5, 22-26

The same principles apply to extended metaphors, such as are very common as parables, sermons or hymns. *Onward Christian Soldiers, Fight the Good Fight, Soldiers of Christ, Arise* are all hymns which, in a transparently clear way (because they are meant to be easily understood by the least literary), develop the same simple metaphor, which derives from the Bible. Yet however extended the metaphor, the only object of real importance in the hymn is A—the Christian campaign. Soldiery, or the manner of development of the metaphor, is of no importance.

A conceit, on the other hand, is interested not merely in A, but in the relationship between A and B. Most often, in a conceit, A and B are not apparently very alike; and the interest is in the demonstration of how they may be seen to resemble each other. It is a challenge to the poet, and particularly to his brainwork. Shakespeare's Richard II, a poet-king, meditates in prison, as follows:

I have been studying how I may compare
This prison where I live unto the world:
And for because the world is populous
And here is not a creature but myself,
I cannot do it;

He admits, in fact, the apparent infertility of the comparison
—a useless one for ordinary poetic metaphor. 'Yet', he says,

I'll hammer it out.
My brain I'll prove the female to my soul,
My soul the father; and these two beget
A generation of still-breeding thoughts . . .

5, 5, 1-8

This is something like a motto for Metaphysical poetry: 'I'll hammer it out' . . . The brain and the soul (inspiration, feeling, emotion) are to work together in the process of creation. One is not fully appreciating a Metaphysical poem unless one sees both 'brain' and 'soul' at work.

Very often, where a conceit is being used, more imagination and creative impulse go into the linking of A and B than into the description of either. Classification is to be avoided wherever possible, as it always involves some over-simplification, but if one must distinguish between a conceit and an ordinary image, one can ask: which is really under scrutiny here, A, or the relationship between A and B? If the latter, then one can most probably describe the device as a conceit. Taking another example from English hymns (which are useful to have in mind when reading the devotional Metaphysical poems), consider the dignified opening:

Christ is our corner-stone,
On him alone we build.

This is a metaphor from building; a glance at the 'architectural' poems in George Herbert's *The Temple* will show how it could be developed into a conceit, with much skill devoted to linking the relationship as ingeniously as possible. But in the hymn it is a metaphor which appears for a moment and is replaced by others; its purpose is merely to tell us about A, which in this case is man's reliance on God.

The dangers of the conceit are not hard to see. The poet sets himself a task, to be carried out as cleverly as possible; if it is a pointless task—if nothing of value is created in all the ingenuities—or if he loses sight completely of the poem as a whole, so that the conceit is nothing but rather easy showing-off, like a batsman practising stroke-play without a ball, then the conceit is an irritation and a bore. A lot of Elizabethan conceits are like this. In the Metaphysical poets, however—or at least in those good ones discussed here—a conceit is not empty stroke-play, but a serious means of persuasion or illustration. The conceits *are* the action of the poem in many of the best cases; one feels that the poem could not be resolved without the conceit, and it develops through the conceit.

Donne's *The Flea* (particularly popular, we are told, with his contemporaries) exemplifies this clearly. A grotesque incident becomes an argument against his mistress's coyness and her parents' restraints. It is all very clever of Donne, but it is more than that; he is in earnest:

> It sucked me first, and now sucks thee,
> And in this flea, our two bloods mingled be . . .
> . . . This flea is you and I, and this
> Our marriage bed, and marriage temple is;
> Though parents grudge, and you, we're met
> And cloistered in these living walls of jet.

(*Jet* refers to the black body of the flea.)

Donne was educated in Law, at the Inns of Court in London, and his poetry is repeatedly argumentative or persuasive. The poetry of George Herbert is frequently a kind of preaching, an arguing for God; and the same characteristic can be seen in their successors. Although the strangeness or cleverness of a conceit may allow for humour or applause, it is also being seriously used to support a case. This is not true of Romeo's or of most non-Metaphysical conceits.

THE ABSTRACT/CONCRETE IMAGE

At least one critic (James Smith, in his essay *On Metaphysical Poetry*) has sought to define Metaphysical poetry by another of its characteristics, one in which the 'metaphysical' element and the tendency to conceits meet. This is the fondness of these poets for a simple, concrete metaphor used in the face of some of the hugest and most abstract problems of thought or awareness; this metaphor does not offer real solution or elucidation, but by paradox or a visionary's 'leap of faith' seems to clinch the matter. It is, perhaps, the later poets, Marvell and Vaughan, who show this quality more clearly:

> with what flowers,
> And shoots of glory, my soul breaks, and buds!

> But felt through all this fleshly dress
> Bright shoots of everlastingness.

> I saw Eternity the other night
> Like a great Ring of pure and endless light,
>   All calms, as it was bright . . .
> . . . *This Ring the Bridegroom did for none provide*
>   *But for his Bride.*

Vaughan

> And tear our Pleasures with rough strife
> Thorough the Iron gates of Life.

Marvell

Here A and B are apparently most unlike and incapable of association; indeed all the above examples make mere nonsense if taken logically and paraphrased. The poetic effect is eerie and uplifting; and for individual readers offers perceptions of mystical 'truth' similar to those of religious experience.

PARADOX

This is a frequent incidental device, sometimes associated with the kind of image described in the previous section, sometimes occurring in the witty argumentative stanzas of love-poetry. In

C

Donne's *Holy Sonnet XIV* it is almost a conceit; certainly it is the basic structure of the poem:

> Batter my heart, three-person'd God; . . .
> . . . That I may rise and stand, o'erthrow me, and bend
> Your force to break, blow, burn and make me new . . .
> > for I
> Except you enthrall me, never shall be free,
> Nor ever chaste, except you ravish me.

Herbert's *Affliction* (discussed in Chapter 7) ends

> Ah, my dear God! though I am clean forgot,
> Let me not love thee, if I love thee not.

Perhaps the most subtle use of paradoxical idea is in Marvell's *The Definition of Love*, which describes a devotion

> > begotten by despair
> Upon Impossibility.

Here each stanza is a brief conceit: the relationship between the image and the subject is of great importance. The more cleverly the poet 'defines' his love, the more devastatingly he makes his point that it is impossible. At least two of the stanzas embody the paradox in concrete terms:

> And therefore her Decrees of Steel
> Us as the distant Poles have plac'd,
> (Though Love's whole World on us doth wheel)
> Not by themselves to be embrac'd.
>
> . . . As Lines so Loves *oblique* may well
> Themselves in every Angle greet:
> But ours, so truly *Parallel*,
> Though infinite, can never meet.

Both these stanzas illustrate not only paradox but also the almost epigrammatic conciseness which is another strength of Metaphysical poetry. In the above eight lines Marvell says a great deal; the brilliant appropriateness of each conceit tells us more about the relationship between the lovers. The world spins upon an axis, with the poles at each end; the poles-lovers conceit is therefore two ways appropriate, in that the lovers cannot meet (are as far apart as it is possible to be) and yet that the 'whole world' of love depends upon them. In the second, the perfection of their loves (not oblique, but flawless, thinking and moving exactly alike—'parallel') brings about their separation. It is because the lines are infinite (notice that when applied to love the word means everlasting) that they cannot meet. A painful paradox indeed.

CONCISENESS

This terseness and neatness is the general manner of all the Metaphysicals. Poems may go on at length; conceits may be developed at length; but if so, then something new is being said all the time. The diction of Metaphysical poets, as will be said in Chapter 4, is mostly simple; when one realises how much they say in this simplicity, it is seen as a great excellence.

Often within the unified structure of a poem epigrams, capable of extraction, appear, and are held together by rhyme, alliteration, and even metre so that they do not seem fragmentary.

> The Grave's a fine and private Place,
> But none, I think, do there embrace.
>
> Marvell

> Farewell house, and farewell home
> She's for the Moors, and Martyrdom.
>
> Crashaw

> True Beauty dwells on high: ours is a flame
> But borrow'd thence to light us thither.
> Beauty and beauteous words should go together.
>
> Herbert

> So must pure lovers' souls descend
>   To affections, and to faculties,
> Which sense may reach and apprehend,
>   Else a great Prince in prison lies.
>
> Donne

35

In particular the endings of Metaphysical poems often show this neatness working superbly. After a knotty argument not too easily followed, or (especially in Herbert and Vaughan) a narrative of struggle and discord, a final couplet or quatrain will resolve all.

> Thou art a toilsome mole, or less
>   A moving mist
> But life is, what none can express,
> *A quickness, which my God hath kissed.*
>
> Vaughan

> But then, alas, all measure and all language I should pass
> Should I tell what a miracle she was.
>
> Donne

This is a characteristic shared with many much more superficial poems, for example, Lovelace's *To Lucasta, on Going to The Wars*:

> I could not love thee, dear, so much
>   Loved I not Honour more.

and it reminds us of the showing-off element which is instinctive in such poetry (even when dedicated to religion), and which in turn reminds us of the way in which the poems of Donne and Marvell and others were first read—in the *salons* (to link with the later French custom) of courtiers and noble ladies. Sometimes in these brilliant endings one detects the invitation to applause.

DRAMA

The suggestion of applause hints at an important characteristic of Metaphysical poetry—the element of drama. This is something which the emphasis on wit, brainwork and meditation in Metaphysical poetry has tended to obscure. It does not necessarily result directly from the excellence of Elizabethan drama; but it is probably related to it. In the second half of the sixteenth century, the English language made great strides; it was generally accepted at court, and, more important, received the attention

36

of scholarly wits and poets who might earlier have spent longer on Latin (several of the Metaphysical poets, even in the seventeenth century, wrote occasionally in Latin rather than in English). Perhaps as a result of this, perhaps for no simple reason, it seemed far freer and more vital than before. Shakespeare and Donne, whose writing years were almost exactly the same (1590-1612), between them had an incalculable influence upon the manner of subsequent English poetry: Shakespeare in the development of vocabulary itself, Donne in the use of conceits and in stanza-forms, both in the movement of the verse line. In both writers part of the secret was their use of the words and the rhythms which people were speaking around them throughout the day.

Donne's *Songs and Sonets* are in many respects dramatic monologues—though they seem to represent the poet's feelings. Most of them have probably little biographical accuracy, and are based upon no particular experience. (This is discussed in Chapter 6.) Each is a performance by the actor Donne (who has often been compared, in his anguished variety of mood, to Hamlet). We tend today to expect always to find what we call 'sincerity' in a poet—an honest personal testimony such as we find in Wordsworth or Hopkins; and the notion that Donne's poetry feigns some emotions and moods which were not his at the time tends to seem either false or shocking. This is another Romantic over-simplification which can be a great hindrance to our appreciation, particularly of pre-Romantic poetry. Integrity in poetry is what seems genuine, true and honest *within the poem*.

So Donne presents cynicism and almost mystical devotion; passion and boredom; platonic love and lechery; cruelty and tenderness; and in each case, he uses the first person. The mood shifts rapidly and subtly, even within each poem, as Chapter 6 shows, and this again is true to the way people converse and behave; in particular Donne captures, better than any other poet, the playful cruelty of lovers' banter, giving way by moments to intense devotion.

The dramatic in these poets is most immediately apparent in

the opening lines of poems. F. R. Leavis has remarked the excitement one can feel after reading through pages of Elizabethan poetry to come suddenly upon Donne's *The Good-Morrow* (traditionally the first of the *Songs and Sonets*):

> I wonder, by my troth, what thou, and I,
> Did, till we loved?

Here, with the exception of the 'thou' and the phrase 'by my troth' idiom and word-order have not altered in 350 years; and Donne's lines, as Leavis points out, produced exactly the stress upon 'Did' which would occur if the same whimsical question were asked today. Someone is speaking from the page; and in paying attention we are not disappointed, for it is a voice with witty and moving statements and arresting ways of making them.

> When by thy scorn, O murderess, I am dead . . .

or

> So, so, break off this last lamenting kiss, . .

have the same ability to capture a mood in the diction and speech-rhythm. Donne's *Holy Sonnets,* where one expects dramatic introductions less (the sonnet is essentially a meditative form) are still more striking in this respect, taking one directly to the middle of drama, to moments of climax:

> Oh, my black Soul! now thou art summoned. . . .
> . . . This is my play's last scene . . . (Note the metaphor)
> . . . What if this present were the world's last night?
> . . . Batter my heart, three-person'd God;

Herbert and Vaughan are equally dramatic on occasion:

> I struck the board, and cried
>   'I will abroad.'

> The harbingers are come. See, see their mark.

Herbert

> They are all gone into the world of light!

Vaughan

The range of mood and tone is naturally not so great in these devotional poets, and they do not exactly act out roles. Yet the dramatisations in the above opening lines are conscious and artificial, being designed to serve religious purposes. The 'I' in *The Collar* (see page 113) is not so much Herbert as Everyman.

THE SENSE OF HUMOUR

Earlier in this chapter reference was made to Eliot's famous judgment that in the last two and a half centuries brainwork and emotion have tended to become separate in poetry, to its loss. Something similar can be said of what we would call 'humour' and 'seriousness'. Most of our difficulty in understanding the word *wit* (see Chapter 1) comes from this. We have become more or less accustomed to the compartmentalising of poetry into categories: light, tragic, lyrical, elegiac, and so on, rather as we allot specialised jobs to people and do not expect to meet much versatility in accomplishment (glance at Chapter 6 and see the various fields in which Donne distinguished himself; and he is not an extreme example). We no longer seek for 'whole men' as we used; and we seem unable fully to appreciate poetry in which the whole man is called into play.

Almost all Metaphysical poems have an edge of dry humour to them, which does not invalidate what they say, but perhaps sobers it, and makes it more reasonable. A Metaphysical poet takes pride in offering his most spectacular philosophical statements in an almost off-hand way; and he tempers his emotion with the wise humour of the man who knows that one may think differently another day. Conceits, of course, could hardly be bearably practised unless the tongue were partly in the cheek; the wit and drama, the bold paradox and ingenuity, of Metaphysical verse could not exist without this subtle smile.

Almost any poem will illustrate this. Herbert's *Easter-Wings* is printed on pages 112–3; some people today simply laugh at this poem, yet the very openness of the device is a sign of humility, and the poem is deeply felt and reverent. On the other hand, the innuendo on 'die' which occurs in several of Donne's love-poems and is noted on page 56, is often missed by readers inclined to take the *Songs and Sonets* as solemn autobiography. Death itself really frightens Donne, but he duels with it, laughing, in the *Songs and Sonets*, and in his Holy Sonnet X is rude to it. Marvell's lines

> And yonder all before us lie
> Deserts of vast Eternity

are grim, but, in context, good-humoured; as indeed are most medieval poems or paintings designed to remind men of their end (the name given to such a work is *memento mori*). The spirit of Hamlet addressing the skull of Yorick, or perhaps its greater self-control, fills Marvell's lines with a tense mixture of fear and wit:

> then Worms shall try
> That long-preserv'd Virginity:
> And your quaint Honour turn to dust;
> And into ashes all my lust.
> The Grave's a fine and private place
> But none, I think, do there embrace.

TO HIS COY MISTRESS

Control is indeed achieved by this sad smile, without involving a cynical giving-up (the rest of the poem makes this clear!). The contrast between this and more recent poetry is well made by J. B. Leishman in quoting a line from Shelley's *Ode to the West Wind*:

> I fall upon the thorns of life, I bleed.

Whether one likes it or not, this carries a note of hysteria, of self-pity, and of collapse which Donne—the most passionate of the Metaphysicals—would have found grotesque. In the seventeenth century emotion never escaped in such a way from the discipline of reason and the tempering of humour.

INTELLIGENCE

We have said that Metaphysical poetry is sometimes philosophical, given to the serious use of conceits, to paradox and epigram, to dramatic speech-rhythms and colloquialism, and tinged with humour. Perhaps the most obvious characteristic has not yet been mentioned: the sheer intellectual strength of this poetry. This makes it sometimes difficult, but frequently of exceptional wisdom and relevance.

Donne was known in his day as one of the most brilliant men in London; his fame as a preacher spread to the Continent; and his Works today present a great expanse of writing in which almost nothing is superficial or sloppily reasoned. George Herbert was a leading scholar and orator before settling to his quiet priesthood; and Marvell was a politician of influence as well as a scholar and poet. The more one reads the poems of these men the more one tends to find, simply in actual meaning, that had been missed earlier. One will rarely find a word which does not have some intellectual justification, at least until one comes to Vaughan and Crashaw, where the ju tification is emotional and variable.

This makes them difficult poets to master on swift reading, which is only as it should be but is worth remembering when you are studying the poems. Footnotes are not enough, either; one has to think through each poem at one's own speed many times, and realise that it was a product of brainwork and craftsmanship on the part of a man more gifted than oneself. Donne, for example, certainly moves at times too swiftly for his readers; Ben Jonson thought that he 'would perish' because he was so difficult to understand, and similar complaints have been made ever since.

But in fact it is often this intellectual strength which makes the poem survive. The great Metaphysical poets have a remarkable critical sense, which prevents them from making glib or pompous generalisations (notice how humble they seem, by comparison with the eighteenth- or nineteenth-century poets) and results in just the qualifications and redefinitions which are needed, sometimes half-way through a poem. Many Donne poems begin with arrogance or callousness, and seem, in the process of the poem, to 'think again'; and Herbert often depicts rebellion or confusion by hindsight—he has overcome his difficulties but is intelligent and sensitive enough to be aware of how they occur.

Readers who suspect that this is a special pleading—an attempt to make the weaknesses of a poet appear as strengths—should remember that, in all the arts, 'easy' work is so often simply the lesser; repeated experience of it becomes a bore, whereas works which are initially daunting become clear and deeply rewarding. It is only by tackling the difficulties in earnest, by resisting the temptation to pass over such poets as Donne and Herbert, that one achieves the deeper satisfactions.

3

Verse

The Metaphysical poets wrote in several different verse-forms; there was no one principal convention, nor were they innovators, except in Herbert's unusually close suiting of stanza-form to meaning. This does not, however, mean that they thought lightly of form: far from it. They often delighted in the demands of a particular discipline, using it with extreme subtlety, and the very variety of forms used means that it is often worth specially considering why a poem was written as it was, and not in another pattern.

THE SONNET

Something was said about the sonnet on page 19. The primary Elizabethan form for the short poem, it is avoided by Donne in his book rather misleadingly (for us) called *Songs and Sonets* (see page 21). The reason undoubtedly was that he felt it to be, for love-poetry, too solemn and too hackneyed. The lively stanza-forms of the *Songs and Sonets* allow for the directness and colloquial vigour which help to make up Donne's reaction against the staleness of Elizabethan sonneteering. In the *Holy Sonnets* Donne chooses the traditional form—probably because of its stability and dignity—and gives it a drama quite new. Smoothness was the great merit, to the sonneteer; even as forceful a poem as Shakespeare's Sonnet 60 ('Like as the waves make towards the pebbled shore') obeys traditional regulations such as the end-stopping of each quatrain, and indeed, of each line. Donne presents tension instead of smoothness—the extreme example is the best-known, *Batter my heart . . .* , which with its fierce enjambements early in the poem, almost wrecks the form, yet wrestles it back to a neat final couplet—and manages by the nature of his statements and vocabulary to take the reader into the middle of a crisis. This was not, probably, what the sonnet form was invented for; it is a kind of offence against a recognised system; but the new kind of poem is at least as excellent as the old.

Herbert wrote a number of sonnets, as he used almost every stanza-form available to him; but it cannot be said that he contributed very much to the development of the form, whereas his stanzaic poetry is, technically, unparalleled. One of his sonnets, *Redemption*, is a famous and deeply moving poem; yet it seems oddly indifferent to the actual form it is using. It must be one of the few narrative-poems in sonnet form.

Crashaw, Vaughan and Marvell do not use the sonnet; it had gone right out of fashion in their day, and was not to be revived till the late eighteenth century. In general, in spite of the success of many of Donne's *Holy Sonnets*, we can say that the sonnet was not by nature a congenial form to Metaphysical poetry, for two reasons: it does not allow easily for colloquial rhythms, and it hardly offers the space necessary for the skilful *drawing-out* of a conceit. Donne's *Valediction: forbidding Mourning* would have been a different *kind* of poem if compressed into sonnet-form.

COUPLETS

All the seventeenth-century lyric poetry is rhyming, and the couplet (each pair of consecutive lines rhyming, *aabbcc*, etc.) is always a popular choice. Lyric poems are normally in the tetrameter (eight syllable) couplets, the pentameter or Heroic couplets (ten syllables) being reserved for longer and weightier works.

The pentameter couplets are, as one might expect, much looser and more violent than those of the eighteenth century. Enjambement (the carrying of one line over into the next), which was rare in Augustan couplets, occurs in more than half the lines of Thomas Carew's *Elegy upon the death of . . . Dr Donne*, a poem which expresses its admiration of Donne not only in its ideas but in its mechanics. As the following lines show, the couplet was not to Carew a *unit* at all, as it was to Pope later: not a link in an even chain, but a twist in a long rope:

> The Muses' garden, with pedantic weeds
> O'erspread, was purg'd by thee; the lazy seeds
> Of servile imitation thrown away;
> And fresh invention planted; thou didst pay
> The debts of our penurious bankrupt age;
> Licentious thefts, that make poetic rage
> A mimic fury, when our souls must be
> Possess'd, or with Anacreon's Ecstasy
> Or Pindar's, not their own; the subtle cheat
> Of sly exchanges, and the juggling feat
> Of two-edged words, or whatsoever wrong
> By ours was done the Greek, or Latin tongue,
> Thou hast redeem'd, and open'd us a mine
> Of rich and pregnant fancy, drawn a line
> Of masculine expression . . .

(Study not only the versification, but also the ideas of this passage, which is a most important testimony to Donne's influence on his age.)

To Pope, the master of the Augustan Heroic couplet, Donne's *Satires* seemed simply clumsiness; he admired the *Satires* sufficiently to rewrite them, in his own smooth couplets—rather like trying to play rugby football in white flannels. Donne's roughness is undeniable, and could be defended simply on the argument that some strengths have their complementary weaknesses; but often one can offer a much more positive justification, as in the following example, and in those discussed on page 105.

The following lines, from the *Satire: of Religion*, are the most famous in all Donne's *Satires*; they show the poet's instinctive use of a simple but powerful image, they offer an explicit defence of 'roughness', and most of all they *enact* the effort of which they speak.

> On a huge hill,
> Cragged, and steep, Truth stands, and he that will
> Reach her, about must, and about must go;
> And what the hill's suddenness resists, win so;

The thought is that Truth will not be reached by any easy flight, but only by difficult and zigzag ascents, as we climb a mountain 'cragged, and steep'. Appropriately, Donne wrenches the couplet about, and makes the reader's voice jerk and splutter. The enjambement 'he that will Reach her' is an extreme violence, which must have horrified Pope; not only is one couplet being run right into another, but the couplet 'ends' on a weak, auxiliary verb, 'will', which cannot comfortably be lingered on as a classical balance demands. Then after 'her' there is a *hiatus*, or pause, of some clumsiness, before the trundling repetition 'about must, and about must go'. The following line delays the natural pause (*caesura*) till near the end, to represent the resisting of the hill, and gives the speaker a difficult mouthful of 's' sounds, to complete the awkwardness.

Some readers may think this to be only an ingenious but implausible apology for bad writing. Certainly one would not choose Donne as a poet of smooth verses; the point is that in his work the tension and awkwardness are meaningful, the difficulty of really hard thinking is presented. The verse here fits the sense, and consequently goes to *make* the sense; and so it is with great poetry.

No other Metaphysical is half as rough as Donne, but the freedom and flexibility continue. In the tetrameter couplet, used frequently by Crashaw and Marvell, and also by Vaughan at times, the rhymes, coming that bit more often (every eight syllables, not every ten) make the couplet form more conspicuous and more carefully observed. But Crashaw's *Hymn to Saint Teresa* moves comfortably, conversationally, down across the couplet divisions, without being disordered; and begins with a particularly strong sentence straddling a line and a half:

> Love, thou art absolute sole Lord
> Of life and death.

This is strong and impressive because of its refusal—at the very outset—to fit pat into a verse unit. The full-stop after 'death' is a heavy pause, holding us up to make us think, where a routine end-of-line full stop would not be so arresting.

Vaughan's *The Retreat* is a clear example of comparatively orthodox tetrameter couplets which are prepared to deviate occasionally, for good purpose, from the fixed pattern. This much deviation may be found in any interesting poet—the neatness of *The Retreat* is its most admirable verse characteristic—but it is worth quoting for readers who have not thought much on the subject before. Here is the second half of the poem:

> O how I long to travel back
> And tread again that ancient track!
> That I might once more reach that plain,
> Where first I left my glorious train,
> From whence th'enlightened spirit sees
> That shady city of palm trees;
> But, (ah!) my soul with too much stay
> Is drunk, and staggers in the way.
> Some men a forward motion love,
> But I by backward steps would move,
> And when this dust falls to the urn
> In that state I came return.

Notice that here the couplet is a unit; each pair of lines makes a separate link in the chain. In the first couplet this is emphasised by the strong alliterations of 'travel ... tread ... track', which hold the two lines firmly together. In the fifth line 'the enlightened' is elided, after the classical fashion, to make 'th'enlightened'; this is found very frequently in Donne as well. The fourth couplet is the most interesting. There is a sort of early extra caesura at 'ah!'; a violent enjambement at the end of the line, and a really jolting caesura (placed two syllables earlier than usual) after 'drunk' in the second line. The appropriateness of this jolt to the metaphor of drunken staggering is obvious; it is a simple but satisfying verse-effect. Finally, the last line of the poem is a syllable short; this probably has little significance, but it does throw rather more emphasis upon the plain words of the ultimate statement, rather like a *rallentando* at the end of a piece of music.

Perhaps the finest English poem in tetrameter couplets is Marvell's *To His Coy Mistress*. There is so much to admire in this poem that the texture of the verse may escape attention; and indeed in ordinary reading it is not natural to isolate one feature of the poem in this way. But when it is isolated one only appreciates the more the remarkable combination of energy and delicacy. Here is the concluding, upward-moving section:

> Now therefore, while the youthful hue
> Sits on thy skin like morning dew,
> And while thy willing Soul transpires
> At every pore with instant Fires,
> Now let us sport us while we may;
> And now, like am'rous birds of prey,
> Rather at once our Time devour,
> Than languish in his slow-chapp'd power.
> Let us roll all our Strength, and all
> Our sweetness, up into one Ball:
> And tear our Pleasures with rough strife,
> Thorough the Iron gates of Life.
> Thus, though we cannot make our Sun
> Stand still, yet we will make him run.

Marvell recognises to some extent the couplet as unit, and neatly alternates between separate couplets and interlinked lines. The first two lines make a unit, subordinated to the grammar of the first five lines; there is a fairly strong enjambement *within* the couplet ('youthful hue Sits on thy skin'). The second couplet is a similar unit, with a milder enjambement—milder because subject and verb this time find themselves in the same line. But the third couplet is split right in two: the first line 'belongs' to the first sentence, the second to the second, into which it runs easily, making a sort of triplet with the next two lines. The full stop at 'power' (end of couplet) restores stability. In four couplets we have had constant variety, *without violence*. The next couplet is a separate unit, but contains a bold enjambement ('all Our sweetness') which helps, perhaps, to convey the effect of gathering up strength and sweetness 'into one Ball'; and the following couplet is straightforward ('thorough' means 'through' but has two syllables, as in our 'No Thoroughfare'). Notice here that 'tear' is phonetically an easy word with which to express violence, and that the two 'f' endings in 'rough strife' help the idea of the words. The final couplet is amusingly bold: a see-saw balance across the lines enacts the standing-still of the sun (compare Vaughan's drunken soul, above). After the strong enjambement, and the alliterative 'Stand still' (two consecutive stresses), the heavy caesura is exactly appropriate, before the final scamper.

STANZA-FORM

Most Metaphysical poems are written in stanzas, and there is so much variety that one can make few generalisations. Rhyme is always fairly insistent; and the more song-like the verse, the more end-stopping there will be, for lines of music do not normally provide for enjambement (as church-goers will know). Thus light and easy, though still 'conceited' in its metaphor, is this verse from a *Song* by Aurelian Townshend:

> See then my last lamenting,
>   Upon a cliff I'll sit,
> Rock constancy presenting
>   Till I grow part of it;
> My tears a quicksand feeding,
>   Whereon no foot can rest,
> My sighs a tempest breeding
>   About my stony breast.

This is an easily-grasped, regular stanza; the lines are all of the same length except that feminine (two-syllable, the second being an extra, 'light' syllable) endings and masculine alternate. In other Metaphysical poems the length of lines and the arrangement of rhymes can vary considerably. Donne often seems to allow his first stanza to *grow* with the speech-rhythm of the words, and then to fit the succeeding stanzas to the pattern created. He is also prepared (and Herbert and Vaughan develop the method even further) to end two lines of very different length with the same rhyme-sound. This is surprisingly upsetting, but usually pleases because eventually the succeeding stanzas turn this irregularity into a regularity by repeating it. Thus in the Townshend above, we know, after four lines, where and how the verse is going, and we are not deceived; and, as in

D

popular songs today, we could fill in any lines whose words we did not know with the right number of 'ti-tums'. But that is impossible with this:

> When I died last (and, dear, I die
> As often as from thee I go),
> Though it be but an hour ago,
> And lovers' hours be full eternity,
> I can remember yet, that I
>   Something did say, and something did bestow.

THE LEGACY

Here we are being tantalised. We probably expect the third line to end with the '-ie' rhyme, to answer the first line; instead we find an immediate answer to the second line. The fourth line has an extra two syllables—and also more or less contradicts, in meaning, the third line, to which it is ingenuously joined by 'and'! A more serious teasing is the magnificent opening to *The Relic*, which seems at first as if it is to be as regular as Townshend:

> When my grave is broke up again
> Some second guest to entertain
> (For graves have learn'd that woman-head
> To be more than one a bed),
>   And he that digs it spies
> A bracelet of bright hair about the bone,
>   Will he not let's alone . . .

That justly famous line about the 'bracelet of bright hair' is highlighted by its metrical unexpectedness.

This happens constantly in Donne's *Songs and Sonets*, where-ever a routine *abab* quatrain is not used. The routine quatrain *is*, however, used for Donne's most difficult poem, *The Ecstasy*; it is as if, to wrestle with such a subject, in this non-conversational way, Donne is glad to adopt a simpler verse-form, as a concession to his reader (and to himself). We have enough to struggle with, without being uncertain of our stanza.

When we come to George Herbert we find that the main conceit of a poem may be embodied in the verse-structure. See the discussion of *Easter-Wings*, *The Collar*, and *Church-*

Monuments, on pages 112-17. In many other places there seems to be no special significance in the stanza-form, except in its uniqueness: Herbert hardly ever repeats himself. As Chapter 7 suggests, part of the endeavour of *The Temple* (Herbert's collected poems) was to employ skill in God's praise in as many different forms as possible. Herbert's verse is comparatively smooth; he seems to scorn obtrusive mechanisms such as Vaughan's alliteration or drunken soul; but it is a verse of much subtlety. Look at the use of pause, grouped stresses, the ebb and flow of colloquial speech, in the wonderful opening of *Love:*

> Love bade me welcome; yet my soul drew back,
>   Guilty of dust and sin.
> But quick-eyed Love, observing me grow slack
>   From my first entrance in,
> Drew nearer to me, sweetly questioning
>   If I lack'd anything.

In the ending of the first line one can feel the drawing-back, and yet another stress follows on the grim 'Guilty'. The first two lines are arresting and chastening; the problem is immediately presented. In the lines which follow there is a lighter and easier movement suiting the kind hospitality of 'quick-eyed Love'.

As a final example, where verse and sound fit superbly and unobtrusively together, here is the final stanza of Herbert's *The Pulley.* God is pouring blessings upon newly-created man; the world's riches are to 'contract into a span' (this line, appropriately, is shorter than those preceding it). But the quality of Rest is denied; if man is given rest (peace-of-mind) as well as everything else, he will cease to need God.

> Yet let him keep the rest,
> But keep them with repining restlessness;
> Let him be rich and weary, that at least,
> If goodness lead him not, yet weariness
>   May toss him to my breast.

The first line here contains a most mischievous pun, uniquely contradictory: the sense is 'the rest—the qualities other than Rest'. Herbert screws this joke one turn tighter in the next line—'keep

the rest . . . with . . . restlessness'. The word 'restlessness' spot-
lights the special sound-device Herbert is using in this stanza—a
repetition of hissing sibilants—which aptly expresses a lack of
ease. Each rhyme-sound contains an 's'; the word 'restlessness'
contains three—to the eye, five! The fourth line balances
'weariness' with 'goodness', and the last line follows with 'toss'.
Notice too that the enjambement here fits the meaning—weariness, tosses man into the next line, and ultimately to God's breast,
which with its final 't' clips off the poem satisfactorily. God is
there at the end.

There is nothing subtler than this in English poetry. So much
has rightly been made of the intellectual complexity, and the
distinctive metaphors, of the Metaphysicals, that the skill and
variety of their verse has hardly been done justice. Yet there is
probably no other period in English during which such variety
of verse-form is handled so sensitively; and the reader who pays
close attention to the verse of these poets is richly rewarded.

4

Diction

Some of the difficulty which Metaphysical poetry may appear to hold today is in the actual words used. But editions with explanatory notes are readily obtainable, and in any case the diction of these poets is in reality fairly restrained, and even simple. They are not as difficult linguistically as, say, the later Shakespeare plays, though the complexity of idea and metaphor may occasionally be keener.

THE PROBLEM OF SHIFTING MEANING

However, words constantly change their meaning; it might be argued that, in the closest analysis, no word has for us quite the same significance that it had for Donne. Most of us will never arrive at a full ability to read the Jacobean meaning of his words rather than modern, because to do so one must know the England of King James almost as well as our own England, which takes years of scholarship. But in some more obvious places we can all make the necessary adjustment.

King, to take a particularly clear example, was a more powerful and central word to the seventeenth century than it is to us. Kings in those days were, simply, more kingly, more royal; Shakespeare's history plays constantly assert that a king was 'the deputy elected by the Lord'. The monarch was the absolute ruler, in ways strange to most countries today. Thus, when a religious poet addresses God as 'King' this is not an empty courtesy, but a description full of glory and homage. Contrast the lengths to which the nineteenth-century poet Gerard Manley Hopkins felt he must go to achieve this feeling:

> *Ipse,* the only one, Christ, King, Head . . .
> . . . Pride, rose, prince, hero of us, high-priest . . .

with George Herbert's 'plainly' saying

> My God, my King.

JORDAN, I

The tautological frenzy of the later poet almost implies a lack of confidence in the words themselves; but in Herbert's simplicity, once we remember what wealth of meaning the word 'King' had for a seventeenth-century reader, there is a certain grandeur.

Most cases are subtler than this, and the only way to discover the full force of a word at the time is detailed study. However, a reader coming to seventeenth-century poetry for the first time can manage very well with a modern annotated edition, and with an open mind—that is, he must be prepared occasionally to suspend his modern interpretation and work out from the context what the word means there. For example, in Herbert's *The Quip*, we meet:

> Then came brave Glory puffing by
> In silks that whistled . . .

Here it should be clear to us that *brave* doesn't mean *plucky.* If we are thinking about words we may remember the French *brave*, also the English word *bravado*, and suspect a connection. In other poems of Herbert we find:

> Full of glory and gay weeds,
> Brave language, braver deeds . . .

FRAILTY

where the 'braver' might allow for the modern meaning, but the 'brave' scarcely could; or this, in *Humility*:

> the Peacock's plume . . . that brave gift . . .

or this, in *Virtue*:

> Sweet rose, whose hue angry and brave
> Bids the rash gazer wipe his eye . . .

In these instances *brave* is twice linked with the word *glory* and every time with finery of clothing or natural appearance. So *brave* here seems to mean *magnificent,* even *showy.* The link with courage, we may work out, is in the aristocratic hero, who was both *brave* (finely dressed) and *brave* (courageous in battle). And in Donne's *The Funeral* 'bravery' is used to mean 'bravado'.

All this may seem rather complicated, but most people do it more or less by instinct, provided they keep an open mind and are not determined to read all poetry as if it were written last week. The same adaptability is necessary, sometimes, in the scansion of a poem, as one reads it aloud, where the accent of a word has changed. In Donne's *The Canonization* we find:

> Or the King's real, or his stamped face
> Contemplate—what you will, approve
> So you will let me love.

Here 'Contemplate', which in modern English is stressed on the first syllable, demands that the stress fall on the second; and any reader who is awake to the movement of the verse will respond to the demand at once and take it in his stride. Again, in *The Apparition*, Donne writes 'Bath'd in a cold, quicksilver sweat wilt lie', where the modern accent falls upon the first, not the second syllable.

SOME COMMON WORDS

This short list is presented, for convenience, in alphabetical order, but you must realise that it is nothing like adequate as a glossary. It is a selection of particularly treacherous words which occur frequently; words that are *obviously* difficult have on the whole not been included.

ALCHEMY   There are many references in Elizabethan and Jacobean literature to the attempts of scientists of the time and of the past to short-cut the problems of life by discovering either how to make ordinary metals into gold, or how to prolong life indefinitely. The science was called alchemy, and the scientists alchemists. The key to these secrets would be the ELIXIR, or

Philosopher's Stone. Herbert's poem *The Elixir* contains the lines:

> This is the famous stone
> That turneth all to gold;

The conceit is that true humility and reverence on man's part are the only real 'elixir'. 'That which God doth touch and own' is as valuable, Herbert says, as gold.

Another of the alchemists' aims was to extract from any material the QUINTESSENCE. The following note is quoted from Theodore Redpath's edition of Donne's *Songs and Sonets*: 'The "fifth essence" of ancient and medieval philosophy, supposed to be the substance of which the heavenly bodies were made, and to be actually latent in all things.'

These ideas are mentioned frequently in Metaphysical poetry, usually with an irony which implies that the writer is far from convinced that the alchemists will ever discover anything. This is the implication of the Herbert poem just mentioned, and, more dogmatically, of these lines from Donne's *The Sun Rising*:

> Princes do but play us; compar'd to this,
> All honour's mimic, all wealth alchemy.

DIE Readers who know other sixteenth-, seventeenth-, and even eighteenth-century poetry may well be familiar with the innuendo which this word can have, coming, it seems, from colloquial language of the time: that is, to 'die' is to achieve sexual gratification. At its worst it may be a poor joke; at its best it can carry an exciting irony and seriousness. That love, the most *living* of experiences, should be linked to death may seem strange; but generations of writers, composers, and psychologists have found a kind of truth in the idea; and the suggestions of sacrifice, and of stepping out of oneself, are meaningful also. A fine example of this is in Donne's *Canonization*:

> Call us what you will, we are made such by love;
>   Call her one, me another fly,
> We're tapers too, and at our own cost die . . .
> . . . We can *die* by it, if not live by love . . .

ELEMENTS The four elements of which the human body was thought to be made, and to which it was thought to return after death. The elements were earth, water, fire and air. A complex play upon the idea of the body after death dissolving back into its elements is Donne's poem *The Dissolution*.

ELIXIR See ALCHEMY above.

GLASS This is reasonably straightforward, but has three distinct meanings, which might puzzle some readers: 'looking-glass', 'hour-glass', 'glass jar' (Herbert's *Pulley*).

MYSTERIES In *The Ecstasy* Donne writes of 'Love's Mysteries'. Care is needed here. A mystery to us is incomprehensible, perhaps supernatural; but in medieval times it meant a craft, a skill which could be learnt. (Thus the medieval Mystery Plays were plays performed by the members of different workmen's guilds.) Donne, coming somewhere between the two, probably felt both meanings in the word; and the use of it in *The Ecstasy* is then seen to be much less wishy-washy than the modern word would be.

PREGNANT This word is so rarely used today with any sense other than that of 'with child', in 'pregnancy', that it must be mentioned here. Its older and wider meaning was of course 'carrying'—usually used of abstractions—'imbued with', 'full of latent significance'. Polonius in Shakespeare's *Hamlet*: 'How pregnant sometimes his replies are!' In Donne's *Valediction: of Weeping* a tear carries a reflection of the loved one, and is therefore 'pregnant of thee'.

QUAINT This means not 'strange' or 'odd', but 'wrought in an elaborate way' (Vaughan's lover sings 'in his quaintest strain' in *The World*); or 'unusual in imaginative power' (Herbert speaks of 'quaint words') or—the one we are most likely to misunderstand—'full of fine and finicky distinctions' ('thy quaint Honour' in Marvell's *To His Coy Mistress*).

QUICK means 'alive', more often than it means 'speedy'. *Quickness*, Vaughan's poem, is about a sense of life, sanctified by God.

QUINTESSENCE   See ALCHEMY.

SENSE   Today this word is capable of several meanings; it was capable almost of more in the seventeenth century. Most often it means 'physical sensation', as in *The Ecstasy*, line 67; but it can be seen to mean 'meaning' in Herbert's *Jordan II*. It needs care and an examination of the context, whenever it is met.

SEX   This word is of interest in that it is used for the first time in something approaching its modern sense by Donne in *The Ecstasy*—'We see by this it was not sex'. Caution is still needed: Donne still means, fairly strictly, sexual attraction, not the welter of psychological and social implications which the word has today.

SPHERE   Astrology, which plays a major part in medieval poetry, is frequently referred to by the Metaphysicals; it is an aspect of their fondness for scientific metaphor, which has often been noted. 'Sphere' is still used by us in more or less its seventeenth-century sense when we speak of 'social spheres' and the 'sphere in which someone moves'. The spheres were heavenly bodies, or heavenly 'areas', guided each by an angel, or intelligence, who moved within it. Some examples set beside each other may help to clarify this; they are all from Donne.

> Then, as an Angel, face and wings
> Of air, not pure as it, yet pure, doth wear,
> So thy love may be my love's sphere . . .
>
> AIR AND ANGELS

> Shine here to us, and thou art everywhere;
> This bed thy centre is, these walls thy sphere.
>   (Here, in THE SUN RISING, the sense is almost *orbit*.)

> But oh alas, so long, so far
>   Our bodies why do we forbear?

They're ours, though they're not we, we are
   The intelligences, they the sphere.

THE ECSTASY

Let man's soul be a Sphere, and then in this,
   The intelligence that moves, devotion is....

GOOD FRIDAY, 1613

The spheres, furthermore, could move, and 'influence' events and each other; much of the science of astrology lay in studying the movements of the spheres. There are references to this in *Good Friday 1613* (the lines immediately following the above quotation) and in Herbert's *Vanity*; and Donne's famous *Valediction: Forbidding Mourning* speaks of 'trepidation of the spheres'.

SUBTLE is one of Donne's favourite words. As well as 'complex', 'intricate', 'not at once noticeable', it means 'fine and delicate', as in 'that subtle wreath of hair' (Donne, *The Funeral*); or 'clever', as in Herbert's 'the subtle chemic' (*Vanity*) or 'secret' 'hard to unravel', as in 'that subtle knot, which makes us man' (Donne, *The Ecstasy*).

SWEET   The meaning of this word has changed, it would seem from a dictionary, very little; its usage and connotation have changed hugely. For us it has been spoilt, and seems sickly, trivial, hopelessly linked with descriptions of poodles or of what Americans call 'candy'. Once again, it is a narrowing and specialisation of thought which has taken place, to our great loss. The delicate, fragrant associations of this word were abundantly present in the seventeenth century, but without any suggestion of un-masculine or feeble feeling; it was both strong *and* delicate, just as poetry could be emotional *and* intellectual or serious *and* humorous, at the same time. We must make the effort to see that the lines below are not cloying, as they would seem if written by a modern poet:

Sweet day, so cool, so calm, so bright,
   The bridal of the earth and sky:

59

The dew shall weep thy fall tonight;
    For thou must die.

Sweet rose, whose hue angry and brave
Bids the rash gazer wipe his eye:
Thy root is ever in its grave,
    And thou must die.

Sweet spring, full of sweet days and roses,
A box where sweets compacted lie;
My music shows ye have your closes,
    And all must die.

Only a sweet and virtuous soul,
Like season'd timber, never gives;
But though the whole world turn to coal,
    Then chiefly lives.

VIRTUE, Herbert

(Note in each verse how closely the metaphors *fit*. Dew *is* wet, and *does* mark the end of the day; the root *is* in the earth into which the flower will finally rot; the 'music' of this poem *does* have dying falls ['closes' meaning such cadences in music]. Note also the touch of humorous wit, in the play upon 'sweets'— perfumes—in the third verse.) As the simile of seasoned timber should show, 'sweet' here does not carry any suggestion of fragility.

It is a word which occurs very frequently in Elizabethan and seventeenth-century verse, often with intense feeling behind it. One more example will perhaps support the point: Marvell's famous lines from *To His Coy Mistress*—

Let us roll all our strength, and all
Our sweetness, up into one ball ...

'Sweetness' in these poets might almost be translated 'goodness', as we use it when we speak of getting the 'goodness' of an apple, or a wine, or a sunny day. It may well denote delicacy and beauty, but there is nothing 'soft' about it, and we must get the poodles right out of our heads.

WIT   See pages 21-2 for an attempt to explain the complex significance of this word for a seventeenth-century poet. In general it is a quality aspired to, but there are occasions where it is used to mean 'uninspired professionalism' or just 'showing-off', such as Herbert's shrewd observation that a man of 'quick Wit and Conversation' must needs 'to be short, make an oration' (*The Quip*), or Vaughan's satirical description of 'the doting lover' in *The World*:

> his Lute, his fancy, and his flights,
> Wit's sour delights . . .

WORK   Herbert and Crashaw both use the phrase 'work and wind'—Herbert of rising flames, Crashaw of 'curl'd Waves'. It means 'labour under stress, heave, twist'—we speak of 'working one's way into' something, and of yeast 'working' in dough. So, when Herbert speaks in *Praise (III)* of 'my working breast', he means 'my breast full of trouble and tribulation'.

SYLLABLES

Most readers will know that in poetry before about 1820 -*ed* at the end of a past participle is pronounced, unless (as more commonly happens) the 'e' is replaced by an apostrophe. In Herbert's *Affliction*, for example:

> I looked on thy furniture so fine . . .

the 'ed' is lightly pronounced; but in 'season'd' in *Virtue* it is omitted.

With 'ion' endings there is no firm convention and one must scan as one goes. Usually 'ion' is one syllable ('yun') as today; in some places, however, it is two, as in this example from *A Valediction: Forbidding Mourning*:

> Our two souls therefore, which are one,
>   Though I must go, endure not yet
> A breach, but an expansion,
>   As gold to airy thinness beat.

Here 'expansion' has four syllables, and rhymes with 'one'. In Donne the 'ion' ending is *normally* two syllables (but not always); in Herbert it is normally one (but sometimes two, as in the eighth line of *Redemption*). In Crashaw, Marvell, and Vaughan the two-syllable form seems to have dropped out.

THE POETS' CHOICE OF DICTION

Elizabethan times saw an explosive development of the English language, which reached its peak in the work of Shakespeare. Words fascinated the Elizabethan poet, as they did later the nineteenth-century poets who followed Keats (Tennyson, Hopkins, even Swinburne); these writers attempt not merely arrangement but also creation—Shakespeare and Hopkins, the most courageous and imaginative of these, cheerfully invented words where they were needed!

To the comparative extravagance of the dramatists, Donne offers a reaction, and Herbert follows. Metaphysical poets are not so interested in words as in thoughts; their use of words is superb, but always geared to the purpose of thought, with absolutely no indulgence in sound for its own sake. One would not find anything in Donne to resemble Macbeth's

> But now I'm cabin'd, cribb'd, confin'd, bound in
> To saucy doubts and fears.

where the repetition with alliteration and assonance help to create the claustrophobia of the speaker's situation. Donne does not repeat himself in this way; he would probably be puzzled by the muddle of Shakespeare's line. There is little attempt, in Donne, to 'build up atmospheres' or reproduce sensations; there is more, but still comparatively little in Vaughan and Marvell; even the sumptuousness of Crashaw works through an orderly procession of metaphor and argument.

Donne and Herbert studied rhetoric, as students, and one became the finest writer of sermons in the country, the other the Public Orator at Cambridge. In both poets there is warmth and vigour, and Donne's rhythms can be compared in their effect to those of Shakespeare, yet there is not the same inflammability of language (the great cascades of Donne's sermons come nearest to Shakespeare in this respect). Sir Walter Scott said that the

Metaphysicals played with thoughts as the Elizabethans had played with words, and this is a good rough statement of the difference.

In neither case, though, was the 'play' necessarily trivial. Perhaps Shakespeare's Sonnet 60 plays with words:

> Nativity, once in the main of light,
> Crawls to maturity, wherewith being crown'd
> Crooked eclipses 'gainst his glory fight . . .

but the result is a dazzling succession of images and sound-relationships which make a hackneyed idea into an astonishingly fresh creation. This cannot really be paraphrased.

By contrast, the Metaphysical poets move towards clarity and precision. Control, and simplicity of diction, are important to them, perhaps because their ideas are—far from being hackneyed —often of peculiar newness and difficulty. Directness, and an appearance of honesty, are valued highly.

Much of this is due to the great use made by the Metaphysicals of colloquial language. Donne is very largely responsible for this; his poetry is almost always highly idiomatic, and the keen dramatic sense which shows itself in all aspects of his work is never clearer than in the sound of the speaking voice, which seems always present. Herbert also writes with much colloquialism; it is part of his deliberate straightforwardness, announced in *Jordan I*—'Shepherds are honest people, let them sing'.

Colloquialism, of course, allows for at least as much variety as a more formal language. Two fine examples will help to make the point. First, the close of Herbert's famous *Love*:

> . . . Love took my hand, and smiling did reply,
>   'Who made the eyes but I?'
>
> 'Truth, Lord, but I have marr'd them; let my shame
>   Go where it doth deserve.'
> 'And know you not,' says Love, 'who bore the blame?'
>   'My dear, then I will serve.'
> 'You must sit down,' says Love, 'and taste my meat.
>   So I did sit and eat.

It is hard to imagine a poet at any other period—even any man other than Herbert—summing up the noble doctrine of redemption by Christ's death on the cross in the simple 'bore the blame'. In this poem it seems to work; indeed all the restraint and humility of the poem cannot rob it of dignity. One pictures host and guest; in the 'My dear, then I . . .' and the 'You must sit down . . .' one can hear the polite firmnesses one hears still today; yet it is more impressive, as evidence of faith and devotion, than all the baroque luxuriance of Crashaw.

Secondly, the opening of Donne's *The Canonization*:

> For Godsake hold your tongue, and let me love,
>   Or chide my palsy, or my gout,
> My five gray hairs, or ruin'd fortune flout,
>   With wealth your state, your mind with arts improve,
>   Take you a course, get you a place,
>   Observe his honour, or his grace,
> Or the King's real, or his stamp'd face
>   Contemplate; what you will, approve,
>   So you will let me love.

It is impossible here to talk about the diction without also talking of the rhythm; in spite of the demands of stanza, verse, and rhyme, this is absolutely idiomatic, and most vigorously so. The first line and the last two (where almost every word seems to need an infuriated stress) are almost unequalled for their realistic impact, outside drama (if you know the poetry of Robert Browning, compare all his 'Zooks'es and 'Grrrr's with this, and see whether the Donne does not seem the more effective).

Yet all the time, it is worth noting, Donne is obeying a difficult little challenge he has set himself; that is, that in all five stanzas of this poem, the first and last lines end with the word 'love', and consequently 'ove' rhymes are at a premium. Technical virtuosity combined with such apparent naturalness—an extraordinary achievement, which has a number of parallels in Metaphysical poetry, and few beyond.

These two basic elements of our language are both used by the Metaphysical poets: the Anglo-Saxon, mostly monosyllabic words, for simplicity and vigour (they predominate in the two extracts just discussed), the Latinate words in order to try to pin down the virtually ungraspable, or to achieve precision. Donne's *The Ecstasy*—certainly one of the most difficult poems in English, and one which significantly has been mentioned several times already in this chapter—mixes the two kinds of language strikingly; we meet 'pregnant', 'intergraft', 'propagation', 'suspends', 'advance', 'negotiate', 'sepulchral', 'refin'd', 'concoction', 'unperplex', 'interanimates', 'defects', 'atomies', 'intelligences', and so on, yet the most profound statements of the poem are voiced almost baldly:

> We see by this it was not sex;
> We see we saw not what did move.

or

> Else a great Prince in prison lies.

Latinate language is generally the more precise, mathematical, and cold. Marvell makes the utmost use of this in his *The Definition of Love*. It is one of the finest Metaphysical poems, marked by a cunning discipline which reminds one particularly of Herbert. Just as Herbert expresses disorder in the disordered verse of *The Collar*, so Marvell, writing of an impossible love fettered and barred, uses a rigidity of verse and a pedantic precision of Latinate language within which, by the use of violent Saxon verbs, he creates great tension.

> My Love is of a birth as rare
> As 'tis for object strange and high:
> It was begotten by despair
> Upon Impossibility.
>
> Magnanimous Despair alone
> Could show me so divine a thing,

Where feeble Hope could ne'er have flown
But vainly flapped its tinsel wing.

And yet I quickly might arrive
Where my extended soul is fixed,
But Fate does Iron wedges drive,
And always crowds itself betwixt.

For Fate with jealous eye does see
Two perfect Loves; nor lets them close:
Their union would her ruin be,
And her Tyrannic power depose.

And therefore her Decrees of Steel
Us as the distant Poles have plac'd,
(Though Love's whole World on us doth wheel)
Not by themselves to be embrac'd.

Unless the giddy Heaven fall,
And Earth some new Convulsion tear,
And, us to join, the World should all
Be cramp'd into a Planisphere.

As Lines so Loves *oblique* may well
Themselves in every angle greet:
But ours so truly *Parallel*,
Though infinite can never meet.

Therefore the Love which us doth bind,
But Fate so enviously debars,
Is the Conjunction of the Mind,
And Opposition of the Stars.

The short lines show up the long words, such as 'Impossi-
bility' (a bleak ending to the first stanza, almost choking the
poem off at the start), 'Magnanimous', and so on. The metaphors
linked with these words are of astrology, geography and geometry, and all imply fixity: the opposite poles of the world, the
infinity of parallel lines which can never meet. So cold a poem,
it seems; yet struggling against this Latin coldness is a ferocity
of simple, passionate metaphor, written with the Saxon strength
of the language: 'vainly *flapped* its tinsel wing', 'Fate does *Iron
wedges drive* And always *crowds* itself betwixt', '*ruin*', 'Decrees

of *Steel*', 'Though Love's whole World on us doth *wheel*', 'Unless the *giddy* Heaven *fall*', 'some new *Convulsion tear*' ('Convulsion' is, of course, a Latin word, but it belongs with the violence here), 'the World should all Be *cramp'd* into a Planisphere . . .'

Passion, one might say, writhes vainly on the rack of rigidity. The neatness of the end—no resignation, but a sort of victory for the impersonal forces separating the lovers—is rather horrifying.

In Marvell's other poetry, and in Crashaw and Vaughan, the diction is still predominantly simple, interspersed with the occasional, sometimes astonishing, Latin word. Best known is the extraordinary

> Annihilating all that's made
> To a green Thought in a green Shade
>
> THE GARDEN

There is a freshness in these three later poets—a lightness and even gaiety which cannot be found in Donne or Herbert. It is, perhaps, a certain naivety, and it may have something to do with the straight-forwardness of the tetrameter couplet. After the sheer solidity and professionalism of Donne and Herbert, the ease of

> There like a Bird it sits, and sings,
> Then whets, and combs its silver Wings . . .
>
> THE GARDEN, Marvell

or

> What Heaven-besieged Heart is this
> Stands Trembling at the Gate of Bliss . . .
>
> A LETTER TO THE COUNTESS OF DENBIGH, Crashaw

or

> O how I long to travel back
> And tread again that ancient track!
>
> THE RETREAT, Vaughan

—the ease of these is that of the brilliant amateur, risking sing-song and achieving clear and memorable statement. Yet again it is the simplicity with which these dazzling effects are obtained which is most noticeable, and the natural speech-rhythm; in these respects Metaphysical poetry is close to the Cavalier poetry of the followers of Ben Jonson, and remains consistent from Donne to Marvell.

5

Imagery

The Metaphysical poets owed no conscious allegiance to a school, nor to any theory of poetry. In the last hundred and fifty years, perhaps with the improvement in communications and the plentiful supply of books, there has been a tendency for young and imaginative writers to join together in their reactions against previous traditions. Paris has seen more of this, in all the arts, than any other city, and London perhaps less; but in this century it has certainly happened in England. There was nothing of this kind with the Metaphysicals—there were no literary weeklies or television programmes, and even the tavern association of poets which seems to have been a feature of Shakespeare's London cannot have existed for the poets discussed in this book. Donne was considerably senior to Herbert, and lived in London while Herbert was at Cambridge, or in Wales, or at Bemerton; Vaughan lived in Wales, Crashaw abroad, and Marvell in Yorkshire. The later poets learned from the earlier poets by reading their writings; but there were no books of criticism or poetic theory.

This is mentioned here because the rough passage through critical history which these poets have sailed (see Chapter 9) has sometimes suggested that they were a revolutionary gang, or else that they were verse-spinners ready to conform to any superficial trend. They conspired together (the charge runs) to make poetry dry and difficult, imagery absurd and laboured. Even the twentieth-century revaluation and praise of their work may imply a band of men writing to a programme, a brilliant theory of what poetry should be. This would be most misleading.

It seems to be the imagery of these poets which has been most quoted in support of this heresy; it is also in the imagery that we can scotch the idea.

This is discussed in Chapter 2, and is important in Metaphysical poetry for two main reasons:

1. Most Metaphysical poems are, at least ostensibly, *arguing something out*, developing a case, and the extended metaphor is particularly suitable for this.

2. Very frequently the case being argued has an element of paradox in it, or of the antithesis between abstract generalities and concrete particulars. The boldness and the irony which tend to go with the conceit are appropriate in these circumstances. As was mentioned in Chapter 2, some critics see the bold conceit 'solving' such a paradox as a characteristic of Metaphysical poetry.

It must, however, be understood that the conceit offers no *real* logical argument, only the appearance of it. Metaphor, in strictly logical terms, is always nonsense; and conceit is a particularly extreme kind of metaphor. If the Metaphysicals were really, as some of their enemies have thought, trying to combine logic and poetry they would be peculiar failures. Donne's poetry is full of ostensibly logical arguments by use of metaphor:

> But since my soul, whose child love is,
> Takes limbs of flesh, and else could nothing do,
> More subtle than the parent is
> Love must not be, but take a body too,
> And therefore what thou wert, and who,
> I bid Love ask. . . .

AIR AND ANGELS

There is not the slightest logical validity in any such arguments; but there is usually considerable emotional validity—that is to say, it 'rings true'. The metaphors of Metaphysical poetry, though often presented—in order to maintain the convention of persuasion—in the guise of logical arguments, offer no development of scientific truth or perception, no more than does

My love is like a red, red rose

or

Hail to thee, blithe Spirit!
Bird thou never wert ...

—and they please us in the same way as do all other successful poetic metaphors, by their imaginative rightness, a kind of emotional truth which tends to be actually quite different from scientific truth.

'Let us hear your explanation; and pray make it improbable' says Oscar Wilde's Algernon, and so might one of Donne's ladies—because poetry is a work of the imagination, creating even when it most seems to be analysing. An improbable image —such as the compasses in *A Valediction: Forbidding Mourning* —if it can emotionally convince, is more successful than a likely one, because it opens newer possibilities, bridges wider gaps between different aspects of experience. The greatest poets offer us metaphors which the ordinary good poet could not conceive, and these achieve more, where they work, than the ordinary 'apposite' comparison.

It is not Wildean triviality that makes Metaphysical poets enjoy the improbability of their explanations; it is a keen creative sense, experimenting vitally with poetic metaphor. The veneer of dry wrangling, which so distressed Dryden and Johnson (see Chapter 9) is superficial only; the seeming absurdities, more often than not, are revelations.

Again, these poets are accused of extravagance. In the strangeness of their metaphors this may very occasionally be a fair description; but notice the control and restraint with which they usually handle their images. By comparison with nineteenth-century poets such as Tennyson, Browning or Hopkins, seventeenth-century poetry is almost severe. In Chapter 2 we looked at Shelley's 'I fall upon the thorns of life, I bleed'—a shout, by comparison with which even Donne's *The Apparition* seems moderated. Those who censure Metaphysical metaphors should look again at some of the popular Victorian poetry:

> For the journey is done and the summit attained,
>   And the barriers fall,
> Though a battle's to fight ere the guerdon be gained,
>   The reward of it all.
> I was ever a fighter, so—one fight more . . .
>
> Browning

> Love took up the Harp of Life, and smote on all the chords with
>   might;
> Smote the chord of Self, that, trembling, pass'd in music out of
>   sight.
>
> Tennyson

> Here now in his triumph where all things falter,
>   Stretched out on the spoils that his own hand spread,
> As a god self-slain on his own strange altar,
>   Death lies dead.
>
> Swinburne

There are excuses for this kind of poetry, which can be taken seriously; but it is hard for the present writer not to feel that it is in idea and metaphor blunted and vulgar. There is a tendency to shout, or else to prattle. Return to Metaphysical poetry, and even Vaughan or Crashaw—the vaguest of these poets—seem beautifully judged:

> Prayer is
> The world in tune,
> A spirit-voice,
> And vocal joys
> Whose Echo is heav'n's bliss.
>   O let me climb
> When I lie down! . . .
>
> THE MORNING-WATCH, Vaughan

> Grant, I may not like puddle lie
> In a corrupt security,
> Where, if a traveller water crave,
> He finds it dead, and in a grave . . .
>
> THE DAWNING, Vaughan

Portrait of John Donne as a young man—artist unknown

Andrew Marvell

Opposite: Sir William Cordell's monument in Long Melford Churc Suffolk. This is one fine example of an Elizabethan 'church-monument'. See pages 115-17.

A gentleman's 'gay weeds' (Richard, Earl of Dorset, 1616)

He left his Father's Court, and came
Lightly as a Lambent Flame,
Leaping upon the Hills, to be
The Humble King of You and Me.

A LETTER TO THE COUNTESS OF DENBIGH, Crashaw

Hardly ever in Metaphysical poetry is there the risk, common not only in Romantic and Victorian verse, but even in Shakespeare, of one metaphor blurring confusedly into another; nor of inflation (the repeated assertion of excessive metaphors till all becomes cheap and hackneyed). Very frequently a Metaphysical poet—especially Donne, Herbert, or Vaughan—chooses one main conceit for each poem; often it is identified in the title. This will be carefully developed, and other metaphors, where allowed at all, clearly distinguished and subordinated. There are many simple examples (Vaughan's *The Shower*, Herbert's *Life*, Donne's *The Flea*); let us choose a complex one, Donne's *Air and Angels*, one of his most difficult poems.

Twice or thrice had I lov'd thee,
Before I knew thy face or name;
So in a voice, so in a shapeless flame
Angels affect us oft, and worshipp'd be;
    Still when, to where thou wert, I came,
Some lovely glorious nothing I did see:
    But since my soul, whose child love is,
Takes limbs of flesh, and else could nothing do,
    More subtle than the parent is
Love must not be, but take a body too;
And therefore what thou wert, and who,
    I bid Love ask, and now
That it assume thy body, I allow,
And fix itself in thy lip, eye, and brow.

Whilst thus to ballast love I thought,
And so more steadily to have gone,
With wares which would sink admiration
I saw I had love's pinnace overfraught;
    Every thy hair for love to work upon
Is much too much, some fitter must be sought;

For, nor in nothing, nor in things
Extreme, and scattering bright, can love inhere:
    Then, as an Angel, face and wings
Of air, not pure as it, yet pure doth wear,
    So thy love may be my love's sphere;
        Just such disparity
As is 'twixt Air and Angels' purity,
'Twixt women's love, and men's, will ever be.

This poem is based upon the single conceit that, since angels in order to appear were forced to take on 'bodies' of air, so Donne's passion, however idealised, is forced to 'fix itself' in the love of the beloved (after discovering that to fix itself in the *body* of the beloved would overwhelm it with excess of emotion). There are subsidiary metaphors: love is the 'child' of the soul, and for this reason Donne first thinks he will be able to 'fix' his love in a physical body (as the soul is so fixed); love is compared to a ship being ballasted with wares that it might sail 'more steadily'; and love is spoken of as finding 'every thy hair' too much to 'work upon', like a craftsman or perhaps a magician. But these, it seems to me, are kept firmly in their place and not allowed to interfere with or blur the main conceit. The considerable difficulty of the poem lies not in the metaphors but in the abstract nature of the ideas, their subtlety, and their compression.

Sometimes one conceit is basic to the poem, without appearing a great deal; a succession of minor images pass over or before it. But the clarity of each image is normally maintained, and the principal comparison is recognised as fundamental. Such poems are Donne's *Canonization*, where the main conceit appears only towards the end, Herbert's *The Forerunners*, or *Man*, where it appears at the beginning and again at the end, or Vaughan's *The Retreat*. A special use is that of Herbert's *The Pulley* and *The Collar*, where the image appears only in the title, yet can be seen clearly underlying the poem, when one looks for it.

Of course there are many poems where one image is not fundamental to the whole poem, but where metaphor succeeds metaphor, rather as a lawyer quotes witness after witness; this is particularly true of Marvell and Crashaw. Still, one notices the control. Take Donne's *A Valediction: Forbidding Mourning*; it is too long to quote, but is well known and sure to be in any selection of Metaphysical poetry. Here the first verse uses the simile of a good man's soul parting quietly from his body; the second the metaphor of melting (and, in repudiation, the metaphors 'tear-floods' and 'sigh-tempests'); the third uses an astrological analogy and the fourth develops it. The fifth uses the metaphor of refining, and that of 'a legal assurance, or transference of title' (Redpath). The sixth compares the lovers' distancing to the beating out of gold to cover a large area; and the last three verses contain the image of the lovers as 'stiff twin compasses', which is probably the most famous image in Metaphysical poetry.

Listed like this, the metaphors may seem liable to burst the poem; but the quietness with which they are expressed, the firm end-stopping of each verse (so that one can move at one's leisure from one stepping-stone to another) and the fact that several of the metaphors are extremely terse, walled within single phrases (e.g. 'No tear-floods, nor sigh-tempests move', or 'Inter-assured of the mind') makes the rational development quite clear, and by comparison with *Air and Angels*, positively easy.

SCIENTIFIC METAPHOR AND OTHER ERUDITE IMAGERY

The 'compasses' quoted above is just the best known of a series of Metaphysical images drawn from geometry and from science. These have been made much of by some critics, as if some subjects were unsuitable for poetic reference; but they are not greatly significant on their own. They should be seen alongside the images from astrology, cosmology, geography and theology which abound in Metaphysical poetry, and which certainly demanded erudition in a contemporary reader. The following points should be borne in mind:

1. Donne's age, and that of Marvell, were exciting, marking great widenings of human knowledge. See Chapter 1 for an account of these excitements. Geography, for example, was as fascinating as space-travel is today. 'O my America, my new-found-land!' cries Donne in his well-known *Elegy To His Mistress Going to Bed*; another licentious elegy—*Love's Progress*

—develops the conceit that a woman's body may be navigated like the globe. Several of the more famous *Songs and Sonets* make similar references to sea-travel to far lands—always with a tone bordering on impudence, as if by mapping the world man were making it his servant. The more Donne mentions the world, worlds, or globe, the more intensely he is celebrating the love of individuals, who

> possess one world, each hath one, and is one
>
> THE GOOD-MORROW

This is extravagant, if you like—the most intimate relationship being 'conceited' to *include* the vast earth, and other worlds— but time and again Donne brings it off.

2. Though one hopes that nobody now accepts the statement that Metaphysical poetry appeals to the head at the expense of the heart, it is clear that anybody reading Donne or Marvell (these are the two more erudite poets) would need to be of very reasonable intelligence and substantial education. Donne is more often difficult than easy. To such a reader the scientific and other intellectual references would be no stumbling-block.

3. Many of these metaphors are metaphysical in the philosophical sense (see page 25). Religion, astrology, cosmology— even geometry—are areas in which the most puzzling philosophical problems are met, and in which paradox flourishes (the round flatness of the globe, the lines which 'though infinite can never meet', the redemption by the crucifixion); and the metaphors drawn from these areas do not make merely ornaments or excrescences upon Metaphysical poetry, but make possible some of that poetry's toughest and profoundest realisations. To cut them away would not liberate the poetry but cripple it.

When all this has been said, it must still be admitted that at times these poets do seem wilfully obscure to little purpose, their imagery forced, and their devices rather manufactured than inspired. It would be surprising if it were not so: most strengths have their associated weaknesses. But there is a great body of work which offers only justifiable difficulties and achieves effects as rewarding as any simplicity, and it would be placing a false emphasis to dwell upon the poorer moments.

THE IMAGERY OF INDIVIDUAL POETS

Below are some brief notes upon the favourite images used by our five poets. Notice how clearly each poet's idiosyncrasies emerge, how personal is his choice of metaphor. This is a reminder that, as stated at the beginning of this chapter, there was no School of Metaphysicals; or at least, that each poet went freely his own way.

Donne

Donne is intensely aware of the physical body, yet of its mystical potential also—its capacity for sanctity, the raptures of love, the trembling of religious awe. The struggle between physical and spiritual accounts for much of the tension in his work. So it is not surprising that *religious metaphor* should be frequently used by Donne in secular poems. In fact, some of his noblest passages result from such imagery.

Thus, in *The Relic*, the lovers are to be dug up in future times and treated as saints. And, in a sense, Donne says, we *have* wrought 'miracles', in having loved so innocently; and his mistress is the greatest miracle of all.

Or, more profoundly, in *The Canonization*, the lovers are not only to be made saints, but are

> one another's Hermitage

—a beautifully tender and delicate carrying-through of the image.

Again, angels are linked with love or the loved-one, as in *Air and Angels*, or *The Dream*.

Still more important is the religious *tone* of such poems as *The Anniversary*, *The Nocturnal Upon St Lucy's Day*, *The Valedictions*, or *The Ecstasy*. Here the talk is constantly of immortality, souls, communion, dedication, or vigil. The following stanza from *A Valediction: of my Name, in the Window* illustrates not only the straightforward religious image, but also the fuller religious seriousness of much of Donne's love-poetry:

> Then, as all my souls be
> Emparadised in you (in whom alone
>   I understand, and grow and see)
>   The rafters of my body, bone
> Being still with you, the muscle, sinew, and vein,
>   Which tile this house, will come again.

'All Divinity', Donne says in *A Valediction: of the Book*, 'is Love or wonder', and the two ecstasies, divine and amorous, are close to being one, in his poetry.

So it is that several of the Divine Poems use metaphors of physical love. The finest case is Holy Sonnet XIV, 'Batter my heart', in which Donne begs God to 'enthrall' and 'ravish' him so that he may be truly 'chaste'.

The most powerful and pervasive image in Donne is that of *Death*. Its ubiquity is amazing, and accounts for the 'darkness' which seems to lie over even his heartiest love-poems. The titles themselves are significant; the following list is from the *Songs and Sonnets* alone:

The Canonization	*The Legacy*
A Fever	*The Apparition*
The Will	*The Relic*
The Funeral	*The Dissolution*
The Expiration	

And there are many other poems in which death or sickness is an essential image. Typical subsidiary themes are the extraction or dissection of hearts (though this is not original in Donne) and the drowning of the world (which will be mentioned below). Any reader of Donne will quickly see how important the idea of death is to this writer; there is no need to say more about it here.

Another major image which recurs is that of *the World*. This is really another aspect of the religious or metaphysical nature of much of Donne's poetry. The lovers are everything that matters in the world, therefore they *are* the world. Or they are so generous in their love that it embraces the whole world. Or they are another world, in themselves—or even two worlds joined.

In *The Good-Morrow:*

> love makes one little room an everywhere ...
> ... Let us possess one world, each hath one, and is one.

In *The Sun Rising:*

> since thy duties be
> To warm the world, that's done in warming us.

In *The Canonization:*

> You, to whom love was peace, that now is rage;
> Who did the whole world's soul contract ...

Developing from this (there are other examples of the image) is the idea of lovers' tears drowning the world, which plays an important part in *Holy Sonnet V, A Valediction: of Weeping,* and *A Nocturnal, Upon St Lucy's Day.*

There are, of course, other recurring images in Donne, but they are more easily explicable in terms of contemporary habit. The idea of eyes fastening upon each other, when lovers are face to face, is found fairly frequently in other Cavalier or Metaphysical poets; and the associated idea of the face reflected in the lover's eyes is even commoner. Rather too much has been made, also, of the imagery of science, alchemy, and global travel in Donne: it certainly occurs and furnishes some brilliant metaphors, but it is related to the age rather than to special characteristics of the poet. It does not lead us to puzzle more deeply into the emotional weight behind the recurrence of the image; or we should be misguided to think we could do so. But the repeated employment of the religion/love association, the insistent reminders of death, and the grand gesture of the lovers' world: these set the whole tone of Donne's work, and cannot be missed by any interested reader.

Herbert

Herbert tries to avoid showing off his erudition, and chooses where possible words and images that a parishioner would understand.

There is an element of Allegory (inevitably recalling for us Bunyan—who was of course of later date) in some poems: *Redemption,* where the parable is of a Lord and his tenant; *The*

Pilgrimage, which uses similar material to Bunyan's—'the cave of Desperation', 'the rock of Price', 'Fancy's meadow', 'Care's copse'; *Humility*—closer to Aesop's fables; *The Quip, The World* and *The Pearl*.

Most important of all Herbert's artistic interests was *music*. He was himself a musician, and in his verse manipulates many effects analogous to those of music. 'Harmony' is a key-word, and *Denial* depends upon the conceit of the soul being 'out of sight, Untun'd, unstrung'. In *Virtue*, Herbert speaks of his own verse as music (see page 60). *Aaron* is about harmony of the heart; in *Easter-Wings* the poet wishes to rise 'and sing this day thy victories'. *The Temper* speaks of 'tuning of my breast, To make the music better'. There are numerous other examples.

The Elixir, clearly, refers to alchemy; *Vanity* describes the astronomer, the pearl-diver, and the alchemist; and *Artillery* refers to shooting stars; but here and in general Herbert avoids references requiring detailed or intellectual education. His imagery contrasts markedly with that of Donne, from whom in verse, diction and tone he learnt so much.

In general Herbert's imagery does not surprise, though the treatment of it may sometimes do so. The frequency of references to fine clothing, jewellery, and flowers fits what we know of his life and tastes—see Chapter 7 for more details. Metaphors of architecture (*The World, Man*, and the church poems) confirm Herbert's constant emphasis on order, organisation and proportion.

One image, however, must be specially noticed. It is a conventional Christian symbol, but the sober persistence of Herbert's employment of it makes it something distinctive: the word *dust*. Man is dust; life, and even death, are dust.

> When th'hair is sweet through pride or lust
>   The powder doth forget the dust.
>
> CHARMS AND KNOTS

> . . . till death doth blow
> The dust into our eyes
>
> UNGRATEFULNESS

How hath man parcell'd out Thy glorious name
　　And thrown it in that dust which thou hast made

LOVE, I

. . . that which was dust before doth quickly rise
　　And prick mine eyes.

FRAILTY

Sometimes Death, puffing at the door,
　　Blows all the dust about the floor.

THE CHURCH FLOOR

The most developed use of the image is in that extraordinary poem *Church-Monuments* (see pages 115-16). Never can this short word have been so grimly and cunningly exploited. In the twenty-four lines of the poem 'dust' occurs six times and 'dusty' once, while the use of the word three times as rhyme-word means that it is constantly echoed, mocking its own echo-words, such as 'trust' and 'lust'. The poem is about the crumbling into dust of everything, including the poem itself, including even time.

The other extreme use of the word is the compression of its appearance in *Love, II*, the poem which he selected to conclude his volume:

Love bade me welcome; yet my soul drew back,
　　Guilty of dust and sin.

That is not capable of paraphrase; it is the most evocative line in Herbert, particularly when one remembers the 'dust' image in other poems. There are several well-known points at which the Victorian poet Gerard Manley Hopkins seems to borrow from Herbert, whom he read and admired; and one of Hopkins's finest lines uses this same image in even terser form:

But we dream we are rooted in earth—Dust!

The tone is fiercer and more distressed than that of Herbert, but the implied ironies and symbolism are the same.

Marvell

In Marvell, Crashaw and Vaughan, imagery and verse both tend to be lighter, more pictorial, less intellectually wrought (with less, one could say, of rhetoric) and more similar to those of the cavalier-poetry (graceful, witty love-poems) which was con-emp orary with Metaphysical poetry during the century. Images inherited from the sonneteers of Shakespeare's day, such as roses, stars, moonlight, sunlight, which Donne avoids and Herbert uses only cautiously, appear frequently.

Marvell shows little of the self-conscious choosing of conceits which we find in Donne and Herbert. His poems do not form sequences, which play many variations upon similar themes, like *Songs and Sonets* or *Holy Sonnets* or *The Temple*. Neither does one feel that the poet has written the poem for the sake of the conceit, which is often the case with the earlier poets. Marvell's conceits are very Metaphysical in character; but they are not as extended as those of Donne and Herbert.

Of all the Metaphysical poets, Marvell had the most vividly picturesque imagination, and his finest metaphors, which he does not repeat, are unsettling, non-realistic creations which may remind us of some twentieth-century painting. The night-mare or dream world of surrealist painting, for example, where abstract and concrete are bewilderingly mixed, where visual puns—ambiguous shapes reminding us of entirely different things—abound, the whole painted with callous lucidity, is in several ways akin to Marvell's grimmer moments:

> And yonder all before us lie
> Deserts of vast Eternity.

> And tear our Pleasures with rough strife
> Thorough the Iron gates of Life ...

TO HIS COY MISTRESS

and, like the surrealists themselves, Marvell will remind some readers of a much earlier artist, Hieronymus Bosch:

> O who shall, from this Dungeon, raise
> A Soul enslav'd so many ways?
> With bolts of Bones, that fetter'd stands
> In Feet; and manacl'd in Hands.
> Here blinded with an Eye; and there
> Deaf with the drumming of an Ear.

A Soul hung up, as 'twere, in Chains
Of Nerves, and Arteries, and Veins ...

   ... this Tyrannic Soul
Which, stretch'd upright, impales me so
That mine own Precipice I go ...

A DIALOGUE BETWEEN THE SOUL AND THE BODY

Elsewhere—to pursue the painting relationship a moment—
Marvell has a warm simplicity of colour which recalls the movement called Fauvism, where a brilliant fullness of bright colours
was preferred to the 'realism' of impressionist painting:

He hangs in shades the Orange bright,
Like golden lamps in a green Night ...

THE BERMUDAS

Annihilating all that's made
To a green thought in a green shade.

THE GARDEN

The real significance of all this is simply that Marvell had an
unusually keen eye—or rather, an astonishing ability to create
very clear pictures for us. In Marvell's poetry, ferocity and
tension meet gentleness and control, the meeting being noted in
language of great exactness. Sharpness, brilliance and lucidity
are his characteristics, as in the agony of the *Dialogue* quoted
above (and of *The Definition of Love*, see pages 65-7), or in:

But with his keener Eye
   The Axe's edge did try ...

AN HORATIAN ODE UPON CROMWELL'S
RETURN FROM IRELAND

Close on thy Head thy Helmet bright
Balance thy Sword against the Fight.
See where an Army, strong as fair,
With silken Banners spreads the air.

A DIALOGUE BETWEEN THE RESOLVED SOUL,
AND CREATED PLEASURE

Now, therefore, while the youthful hue
Sits on thy skin like morning dew,

And while thy willing Soul transpires
At every pore with instant Fires . . .

TO HIS COY MISTRESS

Catalogued, a great number of Marvell's images might appear routine, even clichés. As he treats them, they are seen freshly. For example, a comparison of fair eyes to sunlight, blinding brightness and lightning is a cliché of seventeenth-century poetry—and, indeed, of the sixteenth and early eighteenth (it appears at least twice in Pope's *Rape of the Lock*). Donne uses it in *The Sun Rising* ('If her eyes have not blinded thine'). Marvell uses it in *Eyes and Tears*, with a vivid sense of life:

> The sparkling glance that shoots Desire,
> Drench'd in these Waves, does lose its fire.
> Yea, oft, the Thund'rer pity takes
> And here the hissing lightning slakes.

Crashaw

Crashaw stands apart from the other poets discussed in this book in several respects. His imagery is highly personal, and moves within a fairly narrow range; what is Metaphysical about Crashaw is not the imagery he chooses but the way he handles it; a glance at *The Weeper*, one of his most extreme poems, will show what is meant. If we return to the terminology of Chapter 2, saying that an image describes A in terms of B, and a conceit shows interest in arguing the relationship between A and B, of Crashaw we can say that he often seems interested very largely in B.

He is ostensibly a religious poet, but he makes more impression, and is more generally remembered, as a poet of sensual excitement. Much of his imagery is traditional Christian imagery: fire, blood, jewels, stars and sun and moon, the day and the seasons. But the sheer lushness of his use of them makes the image (B) more interesting and moving than the idea (A); and when to these are added the innumerable images of sexual love, mother-love (with beds and nests), tears, flowers and pain, we are in the direst danger of losing sight of Heaven,

God, Mary Magdalen or whatever holy subject Crashaw has chosen.

In Crashaw almost all cheeks are blushing or blooming or rosy; all repose is in snow-white sheets, or down. Reading Crashaw is to be—to quote a poet faintly related in his method, though of more intellectual stability, Keats—'awake for ever in a sweet unrest'; sensation is whipped on yet never quite arrives; the burning/shivering, pain/pleasure partnership is pervasive:

> See, see, how so on his new-bloom'd cheek
>   'Twixt mother's breasts is gone to bed.
> Sweet choice, (said I), no way but so
> Not to lie cold, yet sleep in snow.

(This is the Infant Christ, in the *Hymn of the Nativity*, asleep between Mary's breasts, which are snow-white.)

From the same poem:

> Two Sister-Seas of Virgin Milk,
>   With many a rarely temper'd kiss
> That breathes at once both Maid and Mother,
> Warms in the one, cools in the other.

From the *Hymn to St Teresa*:

> Love touch'd her Heart, and lo, it beats
> High, and burns with such brave Heats,
> Such Thirsts to die, as dares drink up,
> A thousand cold deaths in one cup.
> Good reason, for she breathes all fire,
> Her weak breast heaves with strong desire . . .

> How kindly will thy gentle Heart
> Kiss the sweetly-killing Dart!
> And close in his embraces keep
> Those delicious wounds that weep . . .

This must all be discussed much more in Chapter 8 (see pages 142-6). Any notes upon Crashaw are bound to concern themselves to a great extent with this extraordinary—some would say perverse—luxuriance of sexual metaphor, which functions, as even the few examples above may show, very differently

from the metaphors of the other Metaphysicals, especially Donne
and Herbert.

Vaughan
Vaughan's world is the brightest of all, the purest and clearest.
Images of light, whiteness and transfiguration account for most
of his finest effects. Not only are three of his best poems entitled
Cock-crowing, *The Morning-Watch* and *The Dawning*, but most
of Vaughan's best-known lines are about light or whiteness:

> They are all gone into the world of light!
>
> (first line of untitled poem)

> I saw Eternity the other night
> Like a great Ring of pure and endless light,
>   All calm, as it was bright,
>
> THE WORLD

> . . . a white, Celestial thought . . .
>   Bright shoots of everlastingness . . .
>
> THE RETREAT

> Life is a fix'd, discerning light,
>   A knowing joy;
> No chance, or fit: but ever bright,
> And calm and full, yet doth not cloy.
>
> QUICKNESS

Even in these few examples you will notice how Vaughan
uses the device of Donne (e.g. in *The Canonization*) and Herbert
(in *Church-Monuments*) of making a key-word a rhyme-word,
so that it will be echoed in sound and have its meaning carried
through the poem.

Vaughan's imagery tends to be the vaguest of these poets, in
literal meaning, though the pictures it creates may be very
powerful. The constant mention of light, brightness, clouds of
glory, heaven, earth and the stars is liable to dazzle; sometimes
Vaughan seems to swim in space, and he has often been credited
with a *mysticism* not found in the other Metaphysicals. His

uniqueness, and much of his success, lie in the baffling and completely unexpected juxtapositions he makes of abstractions and concrete images, or of two abstractions, or of two concrete images—and so on. The process is different from that of Donne's plotted paradoxes, though very occasionally one comes across something of the kind in Donne, e.g.:

> ... things
> Extreme, and scattering bright ...
>
> AIR AND ANGELS

> And all your graces no more use shall have
>   Than a Sundial in a grave.
>
> THE WILL

It is spontaneous (that is, it *seems* to be); instinctive; a flash of imagination, going dramatically against logic.

> Thou art a toilsome Mole, or less
>   A moving mist
> But life is, what none can express,
> *A quickness, which my God hath kissed.*
>
> QUICKNESS

Here the 'concrete' Mole and the insubstantial mist are presented as related alternatives, while the physical kiss and the abstract 'quickness' combine two positive and uplifting ideas into a new third.

'A deep, but dazzling darkness' in *The Night* expresses the 'light' which Vaughan always associates with God even in terms of night. The alliteration—a device beloved by Vaughan—links the opposites more firmly together.

More complex is the amazing mixture of physical and abstract suggestions in the poem whose first line is 'They are all gone into the world of light!'

> I see them walking in an air of glory
>   Whose light doth trample on my days:
> My days, which are at best but dull and hoary,
>   Mere glimmering, and decays.

Here *walking/air*; *light/trample*; *dull/hoary*; *glimmering/decays*
are each, strictly speaking mixed metaphors This should not
worry you, in any poet, unless you *feel* something wrong in the
imagery: rules are made to be broken by artists. In Vaughan,
the blur of ideas is what the poet wants. 'Whose light doth
trample . . .'—it is asking for trouble, and it is the ancestor—or
a precursor—of many crude Victorian and twentieth-century
metaphors; Donne would probably have disapproved of it; yet
it is at least interesting, and at best—for some readers—very
expressive.

CONCLUSION

This brief account of the favourite imagery of these poets will,
it is hoped, show how much they differ; imagery tends to reveal
individual tastes and habits of thought. It must always be
remembered that an image is not the whole poem; the above
treatment is necessarily fragmentary. But probably the clearest
approach to the nature, interests and achievements of Metaphysical poetry is through its imagery, which is usually distinctive, and in which this poetry perhaps records its highest
achievements.

Now is perhaps the time to confess what you have perhaps
already noted: that the discussion and explanation of the conceit
and the metaphor in this chapter and in Chapter 2, though
intended to clarify as much as possible, does not sort out the
matter and exactly explain it. Nor, perhaps, will any other book
you ever read. In trying to explain a poetic image, we are really
trying to pretend it is not poetry; the image exists because it was
indispensable—nothing else would do in its place. Furthermore,
we cannot really say (though I have probably said it several
times above) that an image is right or wrong; here above all we
are capable only of recording our own reaction to the poetry,
with perhaps some attempt to explain the way we feel. Finally,
images cannot really be categorised with exactness; conceit and
metaphor often seem much the same thing, and metaphor itself
blurs into 'ordinary' speech. This is not intended as a cynical
comment on the academic study of literature, but only as a

reminder that you are not alone if you do not feel you *exactly* understand all the distinctions which are attempted in this and other books. Neither does anybody else; neither, certainly, would John Donne have understood them. But it is valuable for us to *try* to give an account of such things.

6

John Donne

Donne is so regularly associated with his seventeenth-century followers that it comes as a surprise to some people to realise that he was born in 1572. Shakespeare and Marlowe were born in 1564, Ben Jonson in 1573, and George Herbert only in 1593, when Donne was twenty-one. Donne lived longer under Elizabeth than under James.

His father, who died in 1576 when Donne was four, was a London ironmonger of some wealth; both he and Donne's mother (who came from a literary family) were Roman Catholics, and Donne must have received a Roman Catholic education before going to Oxford when he was twelve. He probably left Oxford at or before the age of sixteen, since at that age a student was forced to take the Oath of Supremacy, which a Catholic could not conscientiously do. But nothing certain is known until 1591, when Donne entered the Inns of Court, in London, to study law.

In 1596 he sailed with Essex to Cadiz, and in 1597 to the Azores. It seems reasonable to suppose that by this time Donne had quitted Catholicism for the Established Church; Izaak Walton's *Life* makes it clear that Donne had thought much about the matter while studying in London. On both voyages Donne was a companion of Thomas Egerton, son of Sir Thomas Egerton, the Lord Keeper, and the friendship won him the post of Secretary to Sir Thomas on his return. For five years Donne worked for Egerton. In October 1601 he became a Member of Parliament under Egerton's patronage; and had every prospect of a brilliant career in politics.

But, at the end of 1601, Donne secretly married seventeen-year-old Ann More, his employer's niece who was living in the same house; and Sir George More, the girl's father, so violently disapproved of the marriage that he used all his considerable power (he was Chancellor of the Garter and Lieutenant of the Tower of London) to ruin Donne's prospects. He compelled the reluctant Egerton to dismiss Donne, and had Donne, with two friends who had helped the lovers, imprisoned. Even when freed Donne had to go to law to obtain possession of his wife.

Later Sir George regretted his harshness (a sign that Donne proved himself to be a respectable husband), and asked Egerton to take Donne back into service. Egerton refused, perhaps mainly from a feeling that he was not going to run his household simply as Sir George dictated. We know that he approved greatly of Donne and 'was unfeignedly sorry' to have dismissed him.

The next few years were difficult. Donne could obtain no regular post, but still held hopes of a career at court; and lived largely upon the kindness of friends. Meanwhile he was begetting a considerable family. Between about 1604 and 1607 he worked with Thomas Morton, a clergyman in the King's favour, at attempts to convert Roman Catholics—a task for which, after his own decision, Donne was clearly fitted; and in 1607 Morton tried to persuade him to take Orders. Donne refused, partly because he had no sense of vocation, and partly because he still hoped for success outside the Church.

His work with Morton had been too good, however. Morton recommended him to the King and the King came to know Donne well and to think of him as a future priest whom he would favour. Donne wrote the *Pseudo-Martyr*, an anti-Catholic argument, at the King's instructions, and published it in 1610. According to Walton, the King then almost pleaded with Donne to enter the Church.

There was little Donne could do but submit. It is a strange story: Donne eventually became the greatest preacher the Established Church in England ever knew, and the passionate sincerity of his religious work in later years is everywhere evident. But we must remember that Donne's two main reasons for entering the Church were:

1. that he was in financial need, with no prospect of a good job elsewhere;

2. that the King, whom he could not afford to offend, was set upon the idea.

As late as 1614 Donne was still struggling to succeed in politics: he was Member of Parliament for Taunton in that year. The Earl of Somerset, who had been a patron of Donne since 1612, asked the King again to appoint Donne to an important political post. But the King's mind was made up; his words were: 'I know Mr. Donne is a learned man, has the abilities of a learned Divine; and will prove a powerful Preacher, and my desire is to prefer [i.e. promote] him that way . . .'

Donne was ordained in January 1615, and, as promised, received rapid promotion; only six years later, at the age of forty-nine, he became Dean of St. Paul's Cathedral, a position which he held until his death in 1631, and in which he was an immense success. Izaak Walton's *Life* views him as firstly a man of religion, his life being written to preface the Sermons. Poetry is mentioned only as an afterthought, in one short paragraph, as 'the recreations of his youth'.

The last years of Donne's life were therefore, in worldly terms, by far his best; he was a man universally respected and loved (he was, for example, fully reconciled to Sir George More, who had ruined his earlier hopes) and his sermons were major London occasions, bringing the crowds as only football or pop-concerts can today. At one Lincoln's Inn sermon, which may have been typical, 'two or three were endangered and taken up dead for the time, with the extreme press and thronging'.

His death—which, as we shall see, obsessed him throughout life—was the climax that might be expected. He was seriously ill in 1623, but recovered. In poor health from 1629, he fell very ill again in the autumn of 1630, while staying with his daughter in Essex. In January 1631 there were rumours of his death; and when Donne appeared in the pulpit on February 25th, to deliver his last sermon, 'many of them thought he presented himself not to preach mortification by a living voice, but mortality by a decayed body and a dying face' (Walton). He was, indeed, dying, and knew it; the sermon was entitled *Death's Duel, Or, A Consolation to the Soul, Against the Dying Life, and Living Death of the Body*. Early in March Donne agreed that a monument should be made ready for him in the cathedral; and he posed for a painter (at his own suggestion), wearing his winding-sheet and lying upon a board. The picture which resulted he kept by his bedside till his death. Next he called in his friends and bade them farewell, one by one, between March 13th–20th. On March 20th he told his servants to have their accounts with him cleared by March 26th. He set, in other words, a time, after which he was to prepare himself finally for death.

One has to admit an arrogance in all this. The words of Donne's Sermons and Meditations suggest his humility; yet one cannot help feeling that he rather wished to take this ultimate drama out of God's hands, and produce it himself. Very shortly before dying he said, almost anxiously it seems, 'I were miserable if I might not die'; this shows courage and equanimity, but also the realisation that he had prepared his death far too thoroughly to be able to recover without embarrassment. He then folded his hands to the position they took in the picture beside his bed, and died, after the final words 'Thy kingdom come, Thy will be done'.

DONNE'S WRITINGS

It will be seen from the *Life* that Donne's main career was worldly, rather than literary. He published virtually nothing of his poetry, and made no effort to collect or preserve it—whereas his Sermons were prepared carefully for publication. Yet when, shortly after his death, his poems were published, a number of elegies and epitaphs were composed, by most of the foremost literary men of the time. His work was not, certainly, known as well as that of the 'professional' Jonson; but that it was known to poets Carew's fine *Elegy* testifies:

> The Muses' garden with pedantic weeds
> O'erspread, was purged by thee; the lazy seeds
> Of servile imitation thrown away;
> And fresh invention planted . . .

We should note not only that Carew praises Donne for 'purging' poetry (he was later to be accused of having muddied and perverted it), but also that Carew himself copies Donne's 'roughness' of verse; the enjambements of the above extract are typical of the whole poem.

By handwritten copies, and copies of those copies, Donne's *Songs and Sonets* and possibly other poems had been circulating in the London literary and courtly world for years. He was a recognised master, even while, as Dean of St. Paul's, he had almost entirely ceased to write poetry.

Donne's Sermons are tremendously impressive reading, which ought to receive far more attention than they do. There is no space to deal with them here, but the reader who develops an enthusiasm for Donne should certainly look at them, and also at the fine *Meditations*, of which the passage beginning 'No man is an island, entire of itself' is rightly famous. In these writings one notices more than ever a quality seen also in the poetry, a seal indeed on Donne's greatness: the astonishing consistency of skill and inspiration. By comparison, the other Metaphysicals seem almost fragmentary; not even Herbert can offer the repeated freshness of Donne, the combination of conservative stability of expression with continual imaginative discovery.

Few people nowadays read the *Sermons* or *Meditations*, the *Elegies* (love-poems, not poems on death), the *Anniversaries* and occasional poems, or even the *Satires*. For most readers, and for the purposes of this book, Donne's most important works are the *Songs and Sonets* and the *Divine Poems*.

We cannot date the *Songs and Sonets*; but the question must be discussed. John Hayward's Penguin *Donne* dates them as 'mainly *c*. 1593-1601'; the point being that Donne married in 1601 and the poems are widely held to be the spontaneous outcome of genuine premarital affairs, of which Donne (this view suggests) had many. Several poems speak with some cynicism of fidelity in love; the excitedly physical nature of some of the *Elegies* is thought, for some reason, to imply love outside marriage; and Donne himself makes several references, in later years, to 'all my profane mistresses'.

On the other hand, many more of the *Songs and Sonets* are poems of great and tender seriousness, which may well (one likes to think) have been written to Ann Donne, the poet's wife; particularly since reference is made to 'the King', and Elizabeth did not die until 1603. The *Valedictions*, amongst others, sound as if they refer to the long association of marriage, not to a brief liaison. Further, there is no surviving evidence of any of Donne's 'profane mistresses' or of any love affair outside marriage. On the contrary, Walton tells us that even in his student days (not usually the most respectable period of a man's life) Donne was 'not dissolute but very neat; a great Visitor of Ladies'; a wit, and a gentleman of society, but not a rake.

Chapter 1 emphasised the traditions of amorous poetry at Donne's time; and it is at least possible that most of the 'licentious' poems were written of no particular affair, perhaps for mainly masculine readership. This is the rule rather than the exception in literary history. At any rate, we shall not know for certain how and why the poems were written; nor does it matter. The relationship described in the *Valedictions*, or in *The Ecstasy* or *The Canonization*, does not become more serious or valid if we know that it is Donne's marriage, or less so if we suspect that it is not. What is more, Donne constantly dramatises; each poem is a separate attitude (which doesn't mean that it is false), and there is no attempt at autobiography.

The matter can perhaps be put most clearly by saying that Donne would have been puzzled by such a debate.

Another widely held misconception is that Donne stopped writing love-poetry and started writing divine poems, perhaps when he entered the Church; that there was a 'conversion', as there was with Henry Vaughan. The truth is that when Donne entered the Church he more or less gave up *all* poetry. Probably only the *Hymns* (poetry, that is, for Church use) were written later. To think that Donne was a lover and *then* a Christian is another example of our twentieth-century mistake of splitting up the balanced Renaissance man into Romantic compartments; the poetry of Andrew Marvell should remind us how wrong this is.

We cannot, then, date most of Donne's poetry, more than to

say that it is likely to have been written between 1590 and 1614: almost exactly Shakespeare's creative period also. And it is probable that some of the *Holy Sonnets* are contemporaneous with some of the love-poems.

The Poet in Earnest

Jack Donne and Dr. Donne were not, then, two separate persons, and we would undervalue the man to think they were. He is a great writer for many different reasons; but one of them is certainly his ability to express the nervous struggle between spiritual and fleshly impulses. Donne's range of emotion is extraordinarily wide; yet there is an inner consistency. One of the excellences of the *Songs and Sonets* as a collection is the individuality of each poem; very rarely, even when the same metaphors are used, do we feel that reiteration which afflicts all Elizabethan sonnet-sequences. Yet they are held together, and deepened by their relation to each other; the underlying characteristic, which they share with all Donne's work, is the personal tone of a man speaking directly and earnestly.

Even at his most flippant, Donne is not trivial. This is not just another way of saying that he is a great writer, that, as Hopkins wrote, 'A kind of touchstone of the highest or most living art is seriousness, not gravity but the being in earnest with your subject—reality'. *Twelfth Night* fits this account; so do Hopkins's ecstatic nature sonnets; so does the medieval lyric *I Sing of a Maiden That is Makeles*. In all these, as well as Hopkins's 'seriousness', there is a lightness and bubbling happiness which we never encounter in the 'melancholic' Donne. Only one who reads very superficially could find the *Songs and Sonets* rakish or irresponsible. Look closely and it is the earnestness which strikes us—almost a sombreness. Donne is too much of a philosopher to give himself entirely to gaiety.

Mention has already been made of Donne's colloquial tone. It is not only that, however, which makes the poet seem to speak so personally, face to face; it is this earnestness. Much of Donne's 'roughness' is the result of the reasoning mind trying to identify or show as honestly as possible the emotion; there are qualifications, second thoughts, new twists to an idea; and in Donne a new twist is repeatedly a sign not so much of ingenuity as of integrity.

The earnestness becomes frequently a real darkness. Many of Donne's most 'positive' love-poems—those which assert all-inclusive peace, and which avoid metaphors of death or illness—nevertheless carry in them a flavour of pathos, or regret. In *The Canonization* the lovers are, in a sense, on the retreat. 'We can die by it, if not live by love . . .'

In *The Anniversary*:

> Who is so safe as we? where none can do
> Treason to us, *except one of us two* . . .

And even such confident poems as the brash *The Sun Rising* or the quiet *Valediction: Forbidding Mourning* amount to a hope only, an assertion in the face of circumstances.

A majority of Donne's poems, of course, deal directly with *dis*content; with parting, death, disloyalty or unrequited love. And the *Holy Sonnets* are astrain with tension.

> These are my best days, when I shake with fear
>
> HOLY SONNET XIX

Donne's poetry is always quick with fear; and, as the traditional paradox runs, it is the more courageous for that. The religious writings have the darkness of the *Dies Irae* behind them:

> What if this present were the world's last night?
>
> HOLY SONNET XIII

> . . . that face
> Whose fear already shakes my every joint
>
> HOLY SONNET VI

> I dare not move my dim eyes any way,
> Despair behind, and death before doth cast
> Such terror . . .
>
> HOLY SONNET I

'therefore never send to know for whom the bell tolls; it tolls for thee.'

Donne's confronting of death is not made easy by his Christian belief; his sense of his own sin terrifies him. Yet it is not quite panic. It is the utter humility of one close to panic, submitting himself to God's mercy.

> I have a sin of fear, that when I've spun
>   My last thread, I shall perish on the shore;
> Swear by thyself, that at my death thy Son
> Shall shine as he shines now, and heretofore;
>   And having done that, thou hast done,
>   I fear no more.

HYMN TO GOD THE FATHER

(The pun on Donne's name in this poem should be appreciated: no word-play could be more in earnest.) It is complete submission, not through laziness, but through humility.

> Take me to you, imprison me, for I
> Except you enthrall me, never shall be free,
> Nor ever chaste, except you ravish me.

HOLY SONNET XIV

In Chapter 5 it was said how pervasive in the love poetry is imagery of death or disease. The fact that this is a characteristic of several Jacobean writers (Eliot's *Whispers of Immortality* links Donne to the dramatist Webster, who 'saw the skull beneath the skin') does not make it less important in Donne. Even *The Ecstasy*, perhaps his most assured poem in celebration of love, ends:

> he shall see
> Small change, when we're to bodies gone.

And even the warm *Valediction: Forbidding Mourning* begins with a simile of a death-bed.

One of Donne's greatest and most complex poems, *A Nocturnal Upon St Lucy's Day*, comes to terms with the darkness by making it an artifice (we remember that in the days of Wit the use of conceit and artifice did not invalidate emotion). *Nocturnal* means night-poem: it is midnight. St. Lucy's is the shortest day of the year. This is the darkest moment earth ever knows; all life is sunk into the soil, 'Dead and interr'd' (notice the rhythm, with a heavy caesura following). But the poet is darker and deader still; he is the 'epitaph' on all these. He is the ultimate of deadness; his new parents (after love had killed him once) are 'absence, darkness, death; things which are not'.

Negation is piled upon negation. Donne is 'the grave Of all that's nothing'; indeed,

> by her death (which word wrongs her)
> Of the first nothing the Elixir grown;

The death of the loved one (we do not know whom Donne is writing of, but probably the poem was written for a real death or illness)—who ought to have been immortal—contradicts life; so much so that Donne becomes the quintessence or Elixir (see Chapter 4) of the original nothing, before the world was created. The death of the loved one is the extinction of all that has ever been. So it is truly appropriate that 'her long night's festival'— the night of watch over a dead body—should be the longest night of the year: the poem ends with an adaptation of the first line, which helps the feeling of claustrophobia which its repeated negations produce.

This is a very brief account; the poem needs closer attention. Here the fear and darkness are distanced and disciplined, and the main assault is upon the intellect; but the poem is an extreme expression of Donne's most fundamental preoccupation.

His intelligence and earnestness produce other fears and uncertainties. His love-poetry musters courage to face not only death, but also the indifferent world. The fear of infidelity, and the fear of being jealous, recur in the *Songs and Sonets*; while a subtler, equally intense anxiety—that the magic of the love will not stand time or examination—appears in the repeated reaching for religious imagery, the attempts to define and fix the relationship, as in *Air and Angels*, *The Canonization*, *The Ecstasy*, or *The Relic*.

Of course Donne is usually on the attack. He can be ferocious in his cynicism, defiant in his confidence, firm in his claims of Platonic love. Usually, however, his intelligence introduces qualifications or adaptations (the word *Yet* is common in his poems); and behind all we have the sense of a man of high integrity, trying to be exact, trying to be true to the event and the poem. The earnestness, then, is not merely a characteristic, but a great strength.

Good Taste

Donne's poetry is known by its consistent use of the first person, dramatic and conversational tones, a biting and rather sad humour, and its almost savage vividness of grasp of physical life (including, of course, physical death). There is another quality less often noticed: his very sensitive good taste.

This may seem an extraordinary suggestion. Donne has been attacked for tastelessness in his tarter poems about sex, for tastelessness in his stage-managed death, for tastelessness in his choice of metaphors and in his ear for verse. And some people will feel that the concept of taste is in any case a stuffy and dishonest one, a society mechanism to avoid awkward thinking.

Clearly there will be people who simply disagree with Donne, or cannot like him even though they may 'admire'. They may phrase their dislike in terms of 'taste', and find Donne lacking in it. It is worth, however, stating the opposite view.

Donne is a remarkably likeable writer, for one so apparently self-centred. He himself is at the centre of most of his poems, and at times he affects an arrogance which might offend. Yet all his work is dignified by a tenderness towards others and by a wisdom which entails humility. Notice how often, in the love lyrics, Donne moderates his first outcry into a wiser gentleness. Magnanimously and almost sadly, he often throws his argument away. *The Canonization* begins:

> For Godsake hold your tongue, and let me love,

—modulates into the calmer

Call us what you will, we are made such by love;

—and culminates in the invocation:

'You, whom reverend love
Made one another's hermitage;
You, to whom love was peace, that now is rage . . .

Again, *The Sun Rising* begins 'Busy old fool, unruly sun' and the rhythms of the first stanza are aggressively jerky. By the third stanza the poem has been heightened: the world-scale is employed, and the love is far greater and more impressive in its confidence, the language very simple:

Nothing else is.

This is like some moments of Antony and Cleopatra to-gether—'The nobleness of life Is to do thus'. Mischievously, perhaps, but with a sort of kindness which certainly warms the tone, Donne relaxes his anger at the sun:

Thine age asks ease, and since thy duties be
To warm the world, that's done in warming us.

Perhaps the noblest example of this moderation of tone through a poem is *The Relic*. It begins with a bitter flippancy:

When my grave is broke up again
Some second guest to entertain
(For graves have learn'd that woman-head
To be to more than one a bed)

—but moves (after some similar sarcasms about 'mis-devotion', the sanctifying of dubious bones) into the lovely, witty humility of this:

And since at such time, miracles are sought,
I would have that age by this paper taught
What miracles we harmless lovers wrought.

The 'miracles' in the last line almost demands ironic speech-marks in the reading; and the serious, subtly controlled last verse confirms this impression. Donne is aware that the claim that his love is Platonic will be scoffed at; he voices the claim with just enough hint of irony to make it hold, to save it from being cloying or self-righteous. There is a faint pathos here, as in even Donne's happiest love-poems: the love is something too fine to be quite true, or at least to be preserved when translated into words. In the last three lines he clinches the conceit by a sort of throw-away, with an intensity which need not be ironical:

> but now, alas,
> All measure, and all language, I should pass,
> Should I tell what a miracle she was.

Similar throw-away endings can be noticed in *A Valediction: of my Name*, *Woman's Constancy*, and *Go and Catch a Falling Star*.

The tone, in all these instances, is complex and equivocal; this is characteristic of Donne. Much of his good taste lies in the sensitive balance between crude and subtle, sad and happy, physical and spiritual, traditional and rebellious. Constantly he avoids the pitfalls which would catch a less mature poet. In *The Apparition*, for all the savagery, there is no edge of bombast, and the twist in the last four lines, expressed in a less emotive diction, confirms and defines the earlier statement. The saddest poems and the happiest are all controlled by a sense of proportion, and by the thread of irony.

The *Epithalamion Made at Lincoln's Inn* shows Donne's taste at its best. The epithalamion, marriage-song, was a traditional form—there are two very fine ones by Edmund Spenser, the Elizabethan—and it is freshened by Donne, in the directness and simplicity of the diction, without losing beauty or dignity. Here Donne dwells long and warmly upon the subject of the marriage-bed, stirs the blood of the reader, and of the girl addressed, yet speaks with perfect tact and tenderness.

> This bed is only to virginity
> A grave, but, to a better state, a cradle;
> Till now thou wast but able
> To be what now thou art; then that by thee
> No more be said, *I may be*, but, *I am*,
> *Tonight put on perfection, and a woman's name.*

By comparison with this, our age (and perhaps most people in Donne's age) seems simply sleazy on the one hand, or narrow-gutted on the other. In this and other passages of Donne's poetry of love, we find a reverence which avoids sanctimoniousness; passion, without the goatish selfishness of Jonson's characters; and simplicity reaching into profundities. This nobility is met in Shakespeare, in Wordsworth, in the best of Keats and Lawrence, perhaps in Yeats and Chaucer; but it is very rare. It is the right path of feeling sensed among so many possible wrong ones; it is an achievement which no amount of practice and skill can attain, if the great *man* is not there.

As for the charge of tastelessness ('extravagance') in the imagery: the test is how the image works. If it appears stuck-on, a distraction not a revelation, the charge may be justified. But, in general in Donne, the image is inseparable from the poem, and the poem lives through it; nor is the revelation grotesque. The compasses, in *A Valediction: Forbidding Mourning,* do not remain merely compasses to us; they are also the lovers, and the relationship of the lovers is developed as the image develops. Those poems, such as *Air and Angels* or *The Flea,* which turn upon one basic conceit, express ideas which can *only* be expressed by those conceits. With different metaphors they would be different poems saying different things. If therefore we find these poems successful, we can hardly complain of their conceits.

The above examples are of the extreme, most self-conscious images; yet more still of Donne's images are swifter, instinctive, with no claim to cleverness.

> Batter my heart, three-person'd God; for, you
> As yet but knock, breathe, shine, and seek to mend;
>
> HOLY SONNET XIV

> Else a great Prince in prison lies.
>
> THE ECSTASY

> And, in the world's sea, do not like cork sleep
> Upon the water's face . . .
>
> EPISTLE TO SIR HENRY WOTTON

Good taste is knowing what is *really* appropriate (not what has always been thought to be so). Donne introduces astonishingly varied partners to each other—and repeatedly proves himself justified. The appropriateness of his imagery will appear if it is compared with that of Crashaw, or of Abraham Cowley (the 'popular' Metaphysical of the later seventeenth century), whose images are often manifestly inappropriate and so tasteless.

'Roughness'

Perhaps the characteristic which most distinguishes Donne from the other Metaphysical poets at their best is the so-called 'roughness' of his verse. There is, as Chapter 3 said, considerable variety in the verse of all the Metaphysicals, and Herbert several times *uses* roughness or irregularity to represent spiritual discord. But with Donne we feel no sense that it is a momentary device; it is pervasive and very personal.

It appears in several ways. Most common, perhaps, is an awkwardness for the reader in determining where the stresses fall in a certain line or lines. 'Instead of writing poetry,' Dr. Johnson wrote (see Chapter 9), 'they only wrote verses, and very often such verses as stood the trial of the finger better than of the ear; for the modulation was so imperfect, that they were only found to be verses by counting the syllables.'

Thus, in *The Relic*, the line—

Thou shalt be a Mary Magdalen, and I . . .

—is theoretically an iambic pentameter ('be a' elided to make one syllable), but in practice fits into no natural verse-form we know, because of the awkwardness of the proper name. This occasionally happens in most poets; in Donne it happens often, and he seems not to care. Admittedly it is likely to worry a modern reader only in the *Satires*; there Donne makes little attempt to fit the wrestlings of his thought and invective into the comparatively rigid form of the heroic couplet, and the result is a jerky and uneasy 'sprung rhythm' which can in fact be defended as appropriate to the splenetic statements of the poetry. In the

104

Songs and Sonets there is little real roughness, perhaps because the stanza-form is moulded by Donne to fit the rhythms of at least one stanza per poem.

But there is more to be said. We have already noticed the colloquial opening of *The Good Morrow*:

> I wonder, by my troth, what thou, and I,
> Did, till we loved?

If this is 'roughness', it is not something we wish away. Look at another, subtler example; this also, incidentally refutes the theory that good iambic lines cannot be made entirely of monosyllables:

> O more than Moon
> Draw not up seas to drown me in thy sphere,
> Weep me not dead, in thine arms, but forbear
> To teach the sea, what it may do too soon;

A VALEDICTION: OF WEEPING

Here there may seem to be no difficulty of rhythm, the alliteration of the first two lines gathering the thought with some magnificence. Yet the third line is not so easy. Are the stresses on *Weep*, *dead*, and *arms*, or on *me*, *dead*, and *thine* (with a mild stress on *arms*)? The first group seems more obvious (though it makes the line dactylic not iambic); but the second is almost more rewarding. The conceit is that by weeping the lovers may drown themselves; what a sadly ironic way of dying, Donne says—*me* of all people (I'm your lover) to die in *thine* arms (the place I should be safest). This reading captures a fervent colloquial statement which otherwise lies hidden.

The line should be read, if possible, with a suggestion of both rhythms; it will be slow, even halting, but far richer in meaning. Roughness is not unwelcome if it gives us more than smoothness does.

This, in fact, is the essence of the defence of Donne. He seems more or less incapable of the smooth, perfect epigram like this of Waller:

Give me but what this riband bound;
Take all the rest the sun goes round.

But he is equally incapable of glibness and conventionality, which Waller cannot escape. A more challenging comparison might be with Marvell, whose verse has a mid-seventeenth-century smoothness without being glib or conventional. Marvell certainly achieves excellences we do not look to find in Donne; but the converse is more than equally true. In the unexpected colloquial emphases, the jolts and shifts of Donne's verse, there is a constant wide-awakeness of feeling and ear which is of a Shakespearean kind, and which few modern readers will choose to exchange.

CONCLUSION

Donne is without question one of the very greatest English writers; and it is quite impossible to write adequately about him here. The body of his work is too great, its range too broad, its achievement too complex. Furthermore, for all his distinctiveness, the man is inscrutable. His story would be fascinating even if his writings were unrewarding; and there is every indication that he was not only a major writer, but a great and good man. He must at moments have wondered whether his apparently catastrophic marriage had not been a mistake; typically, he brought the thing out in the open in the well-known, wry little pun he wrote for his wife shortly afterwards:

John Donne—Ann Donne—Un-done.

But he seems to have been a steady and tender husband; his relationships with his noble employers seem to have been excellent, even his father-in-law being reconciled to him; and yet his poetry furnishes much evidence of vigour and scorn.

All this chapter has done is to point to some of the most important features of Donne and his work; the rest is for longer books, and your reading. There is, in fact, little hope of our ever doing Donne justice; it may be some consolation that we are nearer to doing so in this century than ever before. The great danger is that we should ever think we have 'got' Donne—

ultimately comprehended him, exhausted what he has to offer, placed him—as might be done with, say, Thomas Gray or even (though not easily) with George Herbert. Of all English writers Donne is one of the hardest to 'know', because there is so much of him, and because he is an instinctive dramatist. There is nowhere in his work where we can be sure we have the whole, or the true Donne; he is too representative of the human drama for that to be possible.

7

George Herbert

George Herbert was born in 1593 into one of the most aristocratic families of the Welsh Border Country. He was the fifth son; the eldest, Edward (1583-1648), was a leading statesman, philosopher, and poet, and in 1629 received the title of Lord Herbert of Cherbury. Magdalen Herbert, the mother of George and Edward, was a close friend of John Donne, and the children —the two poets, at least—were obviously influenced by him.

George was educated at Westminster School and at Trinity College, Cambridge. At Cambridge he became a Fellow of his College in 1616, Reader in Rhetoric in 1618, and Public Orator from 1620: an important post which he held, at any rate officially, till 1627. In 1624 he became Member of Parliament for Montgomery; but in the same year he was granted leave of absence from his Cambridge post, took a share of the living at Lladinam, Montgomery, and already began to turn his attentions towards the Church. In 1626 he was ordained deacon; the next two years are undocumented, but he was probably living quietly, in uncertain health, with friends, and writing poetry. In March 1629 he was married to Jane Danvers, a cousin of Herbert's friend the Earl of Danby, and went to live at her house. In April 1630 he accepted the living of Bemerton, near Salisbury; in September he was ordained priest.

Less than three years later he died; but they were three years of extraordinary diligence and devotion, in which he seems to have made an exceptional impression on his parishioners. Walton's *Life* contains several anecdotes and incidents which suggest a firm and cheerful character, very consistent in its humility.

It is a less exciting life than that of Donne. Herbert did not, as far as we know, travel abroad; he did not sacrifice his worldly hopes in a secret marriage; he actually renounced the limelight of the Orator's post at Cambridge for the eventual lowliness of a country priesthood. But it is important to remember Herbert's brilliance, his aristocratic background, and his probable worldly ambition. He was like Donne in entering the Church only after the decline (we do not know the details) of his secular prospects. Walton, who writes of Herbert almost as of a saint, nevertheless makes the poet's early ambition clear.

> In this time of being Orator, he had learnt to understand the Italian, Spanish, and French tongues very perfectly hoping, that as his predecessors, so he might in time attain the place of a *Secretary of State*, he being at that time very high in the King's favour.

Whatever his personal inclinations (and both Walton and Herbert himself say how much he liked courtly ways, fine clothes, noble conversation), a career at court, or in politics, would be expected of him by his family; indeed, it was unusual for someone as well-born as he to enter the Church, and still more so that he should accept a humble position there.

We shall not understand Herbert if we fail to recognise his intellectual and courtly abilities. On the other hand, it must not be thought that he underwent a sudden religious conversion, which caused him to renounce one way of life for another. Herbert wrote to Sir John Danvers in 1618 (two years before being appointed Public Orator) that he was 'setting foot into Divinity, to lay the platform of my future life'. He seems to have hoped to combine a secular career and a religious life: when deciding to accept the post of University Orator, if it were offered him, he wrote that a friend feared 'I have not fully resolved of the matter, since this place being civil [i.e. secular] may divert me too much from Divinity, at which, not without cause, he thinks I aim; but, I have wrote him back, that this dignity hath no such earthiness in it but it may be very well joined with Heaven'. Later, when Danvers and others of

Herbert's friends lost the favour of the King (1624), and Herbert's prospects were therefore dimmed, he could tell himself—without, I think, sour grapes being implied—that the Court 'is made up of Fraud, and Titles and Flattery, and many other such empty, imaginary, painted Pleasures . . . but in God and his service is a fulness of all joy and pleasure'.

As with Donne, circumstances drew him into the Church; but he did feel the wish and readiness to be a clergyman, which Donne did not. Significantly, we have no secular poems by Herbert; perhaps he never wrote any.

HERBERT'S WRITINGS

He published no poetry during his lifetime. From his death-bed he sent his volume of collected poems, *The Temple*, to his close friend Nicholas Ferrar (who had renounced the worldly life rather before Herbert and set up a retreat at Little Gidding in Bedfordshire), asking Ferrar to read it and then either publish it or burn it. Since Ferrar would certainly not have burned the book, this shows a readiness to publish once Herbert himself was dead and could seem to take no glory from its appearance; and the book actually shows the most careful planning: it is an artistic creation in itself.

Throughout Herbert's work we can see how important to his religion and personality was the concept of Form. Harmony and order represented God and goodness. Accordingly, the book itself is a most careful structure: an emblem of a temple.

It begins, after a short Dedication to God, with *The Church Porch*—the longest poem in the book, which offers detailed teaching to prepare the reader for the temple. *The Church* follows, including *The Altar, The Sacrifice,* and the *Thanksgiving*. Then follow several groups of poems on ceremonies, holy days, and Herbert's reliance on God for inspiration (*Jordan, Employment*); and a further group describing aspects of the interior of the temple (*Church-Monuments, Church-Musick, Church Lock-and-Key*). The last five poems are *Death, Doomsday, Judgment, Heaven* and *Love*; the traditional last-things, with *Love*—perhaps his finest poem—as a most significant close.

Ingenuity

Herbert's poems have an appearance of simplicity; yet they are technically some of the most complex in English. Cleverness with words, after the years of celebrity at Cambridge, was almost an instinct to Herbert; and he obviously enjoyed being clever in his poetry, provided the cleverness was to the greater glory of God, not of himself (this is perhaps why the cleverness is so unobtrusive). Herbert himself said: 'Religion does not banish Mirth, but only moderates, and sets rules to it.' ('Mirth' meant not laughter or frivolity, but an enjoyment of decoration, brightness, skill in the arts—things which a Puritan divine might have censured.) Thus ingenuity is a speciality of *The Temple*. As the poet wrote in what seems to be a late poem, *The Forerunners*: 'My God must have my best, ev'n all I had.'

Herbert is particularly good at the ingenious application of what might seem—in some hands—paltry devices. He uses each device *only once* (we see again how consciously prepared as a book *The Temple* was).

To list and describe all these would take far too long. Here are a few examples:

A Wreath intertwines the lines, thus:

> A wreathed garland of deserved praise,
> Of praise deserved, unto Thee I give,
> I give to thee, Who knowest all my ways,
> My crooked winding ways ...

(And so on throughout the poem.)

Anagram, for what it is worth, may be quoted in full:

> How well her name an ARMY doth present,
> In whom the Lord of Hosts did pitch his tent!

The Water-Course offers the reader alternatives:

> ... If troubles overtake thee, do not wail;
> For who can look for less that loveth $\begin{cases} \text{life?} \\ \text{strife?} \end{cases}$
> ... That so in pureness thou mayst Him adore
> Who gives to man, as He sees fit $\begin{cases} \text{Salvation.} \\ \text{Damnation.} \end{cases}$

Notice here, as in all Herbert's better device-poems, that the device is achieving something worthwhile—putting a point ordinary verse could not do so well.

In *Paradise*, a 'paring-poem' where each rhyme in a verse is a 'pruned' version of its predecessor, the poet asks God to be severe with him, to 'prune and pare' him with his knife, so that

> Such sharpness shows the sweetest FREND:
> Such cuttings rather heal than REND:
> And such beginnings touch their END.

Typically, Herbert has included a little extra subtlety here by ending the poem with the very word 'end'. In the same way, *Denial* (a moving poem even if one dislikes devices) uses the device of broken and unrhymed lines at the end of each verse, to suggest frustration, but finally (with God's 'favours granting my request') finds harmony:

> They and my mind may chime,
>   And mend my rhyme.

The word 'rhyme' *is* the long-awaited rhyme-word.

As further examples of this ingenuity, three of Herbert's greatest poems, referred to in earlier chapters, will now be printed in full. They are all examples of what is called 'the poem as hieroglyph'; that is, the poem acting, in its own structure and detail, as a conceit or image for what is under discussion. The easiest to appreciate is *Easter-Wings*.

> Lord, who createdst man in wealth and store,
>   Though foolishly he lost the same,
>   Decaying more and more,
>   Till he became
>   Most poor:
>   With thee
>   O let me rise
>   As larks, harmoniously,
>   And sing this day thy victories:
> Then shall the fall further the flight in me.

My tender age in sorrow did begin:
    And still with sicknesses and shame
        Thou didst so punish sin
            That I became
                Most thin.
                With thee
            Let me combine
        And feel this day thy victory:
    For, if I imp my wing on thine,
Affliction shall advance the flight in me.

This needs no comment (except to quote Helen Gardner's note on 'imp': 'to engraft feathers in a damaged wing') *provided* that you read the poem carefully thinking about the meaning, and note how the pictorial device fits it exactly.

A more complex poem—some think it Herbert's best—is *The Collar*.

I struck the board, and cried, No more.
            I will abroad.
    What? shall I ever sigh and pine?
My lines and life are free: free as the road,
    Loose as the wind, as large as store.
        Shall I be still in suit?
    Have I no harvest but a thorn
    To let me blood, and not restore
    What I have lost with cordial fruit?
        Sure there was wine
Before my sighs did dry it: there was corn
    Before my tears did drown it.
    Is the year only lost to me?
        Have I no bays to crown it?
No flowers, no garlands gay? all blasted?
        All wasted?
    No so, my heart: but there is fruit,
        And thou hast hands.
    Recover all thy sigh-blown age
On double pleasures: leave thy cold dispute
Of what is fit, and not. Forsake thy cage,

Thy rope of sands,
Which petty thoughts have made, and made to thee
Good cable, to enforce and draw,
And be thy law,
While thou didst wink and wouldst not see.
Away; take heed:
I will abroad.
Call in thy death's-head there: tie up thy fears.
He that forbears
To suit and serve his need,
Deserves his load.
But as I rav'd and grew more fierce and wild
At every word,
Methought I heard one calling, *Child!*
And I replied, *My Lord.*

The meaning of some lines is not easy to grasp. A good edition will offer some explanation (Douglas Brown's *Selected Poems of George Herbert* is particularly recommended on this poem); but also the truth is that Herbert means it to be rather confusing. The speaker is rebelling, with great violence, against God's authority; God is presented as a father, and the poet wants to leave home ('board' in the first line means 'table', a similar humble image to that of the famous *Love* poem, where the poet eats at God's table; but there is also a suggestion of 'altar', which would imply that the rebel is a priest and his action sacrilegious). The whole poem is a (planned) depiction of disorder. (Musicians might compare the Representation of Chaos at the beginning of Haydn's *Creation*.)

After religious images of 'harvest', 'thorn', 'blood', 'fruit', 'wine', 'corn' and 'flowers', thrown around in some confusion, one meets the almost crazy mixtures of 'sigh-blown', 'cold dispute', 'cage', 'rope of sands'. Douglas Brown comments: 'he can't even make a sensible metaphor now, who once taught rhetoric at Cambridge'. This is studied bad writing; for all its serious intention it must have given Herbert some amusement to create.

The verse of the poem enacts disorder. Notice that the first rhyme which reaches our ears (board—abroad) seems to have been misplaced upon the page; it seems like part of a jumbled stanza. And so the poem struggles on. The first ten lines (of varying lengths and four different indentations upon the page) rhyme as follows: *abcbadeadc*.

Throughout the poem one keeps thinking a stanza-form is lurking somewhere within, but it can't be grasped. The music of the poem (to use a metaphor well understood by Herbert himself) flounders in search of its key, until the last four lines where, with the submission of the rebel to God, the music resolves itself, and the very Herbertian stanza-form becomes clear. It is a much more complex example of the method used in *Denial*. The structure of the poem offers a *representation* of what it is trying to communicate. It is as if a telephone kiosk were built in the shape of a telephone—only the poetic use of the device is far more valuable.

For the present writer, the finest hieroglyph of all is *Church-Monuments*. The American critic, Yvor Winters, has described it as Herbert's 'greatest poem', and its comparative neglect by the compilers of anthologies is puzzling. Here it is, set out on the page as it is set out in Herbert's manuscripts:

> While that my soul repairs to her devotion,
> Here I intomb my flesh, that it betimes
> May take acquaintance of this heap of dust
> To which the blast of Death's incessant motion,
> Fed with the exhalation of our crimes,
> Drives all at last. Therefore I gladly trust
> My body to this school, that it may learn
> To spell his elements, and find his birth
> Written in dusty heraldry and lines;
> Which dissolution sure doth best discern,
> Comparing dust with dust, and earth with earth.
> These laugh at jet and marble, put for signs
> To sever the good fellowship of dust,
> And spoil the meeting: what shall point out them,
> When they shall bow, and kneel, and fall down flat
> To kiss those heaps which now they have in trust?
> Dear flesh, while I do pray, learn here thy stem
> And true descent, that, when thou shalt grow fat,

And wanton in thy cravings, thou mayst know
That flesh is but the glass which holds the dust
That measures all our time; which also shall
Be crumpled into dust. Mark here below
How tame these ashes are, how free from lust,—
That thou mayst fit thyself against thy fall.

The church-monuments are tombs, slabs or effigies, all o
which strive to commemorate people now dead. They can be
seen in almost any church. Herbert is kneeling to pray; his *soul*
is going to be busy, how can he occupy his flesh? (It is rather
like the problem of a parent with a child.) His idea is to kneel in
front of the church-monuments, so that while his soul is at 'her
devotion', the body may learn from the tombs the lesson of
mortality, to which our own sin leads us all. 'These' in line
twelve probably means 'earth' and 'dust'; they see the absurdity
of the monuments in attempting to memorialise people and by
so doing 'to sever the good fellowship of dust'. Even the monuments themselves, says Herbert, will eventually crumble ('fall
down flat'). Here the flesh will learn its 'stem' (origin) and 'true
descent' (a pun: ancestry *and* eventual downfall) so that, if
tempted by earthly cravings, it will be reminded that everything
—the flesh, the glass and time itself—will finally be dust. Have
a look, Herbert says to his body, at these 'ashes' of past bodies;
they know nothing of earthly appetites; and prepare yourself for
your end (*or* fortify yourself against a fall into sin; both meanings are implied).

In most modern editions the poem is printed in six-line
stanzas; if you look at the rhymes you will see that this is logical.
Yet none of the 'stanzas' is end-stopped; in every case there is a
strong run-on into the next line. Look next at the sentences:
only three end at the end of a line, and there are many considerable enjambements, helping to pull the 'stanzas' apart—it is
impossible to delay at the ends of lines 2, 6, 15, 17, 18 and
21, and even most other lines allow for only a slight pause.
What is more, there is considerable internal rhyme, which may
seem trivial but is most disconcerting to the already struggling
listener: *blast/last* (linking by assonance with *dust* and *trust*);

exhalation/motion; dusty/dust/dust; earth/earth; bow/now; they/ pray; that/fat; all/fall; dust/dust; time/tame.

The poem is a *memento mori*, a reminder of dissolution and death, like the skulls which seventeenth-century pictures show being used as paper-weights. Everything, the poem says, passes, including the solid monument, including even poem and poet. And the poem represents this dissolution. There *are* stanzas, but they are collapsing, as are even the lines; and all the time the word 'dust' (with the phrase 'dust to dust' from the Christian funeral which it clearly implies) is echoing throughout the poem—seven times, plus the reminders of it which are given by the rhyming words. Eventually even sentence-structure collapses, into a 'house-that-Jack-built' of linked relative clauses: '... thou mayst know That flesh is but the glass which holds the dust That measures all our time; which also shall Be crumbled into dust.'

Each relative clause seems as if it is the final one; the next comes as a shock, which drags us to a horrified understanding of the idea: even time decays.

The poem is made perfect by the sardonic humour (a characteristic of the age, you will remember; but Herbert moderates it with superb control) of such phrases as 'this school', 'intomb', 'take acquaintance', and 'the good fellowship of dust'. As a last touch (compare what was above noted in *Denial* and *Paradise*), Herbert arranges for the poem to end on the very 'final' word 'fall'. On the strength of poems such as this, Herbert has claim to be considered the finest craftsman in English poetry. His 'ideas' (like the 'tunes' of Mozart) are almost commonplace; his working-out of them unbeatable.

'Brave Language, Braver Deeds'

For all its complexity, *Church-Monuments* is predominantly monosyllabic, and the vocabulary simple. The finest 'cleverness' of Herbert's work is the simplicity with which he writes, and the way his technical feats are camouflaged. Humility was instinctive and essential to him; and in the well-known *Jordan* poems, two in number, he writes his poetic manifesto. This can best be summed up by a line from another poem, *The Fore-runners*:

And if I please Him, I write fine and witty.

Whatever he says, however, Herbert was not really content to offer God mere sincere feeling—as the previous pages have indicated. The truth is not that Herbert abandoned the rhetorical skills he had mastered in his Cambridge years, but that he managed to reconcile them perfectly with his desire to write humble, direct, easily comprehensible poetry. No more examples of this will be offered here; it is safe to say that any poem of Herbert's illustrates it.

A much more difficult matter for Herbert was the reconciliation of his aptitude and liking for courtly or at least noble society with his decision to be a country priest. It was his own voluntary decision, and one does not feel in *The Temple* any sense that it was a wrong one; on the contrary, one feels that Herbert must have been almost an ideal priest, and that his poetry represents confidence and stability. But perhaps the reason one feels he would have been such a good priest is that, when all this is said, he has human difficulties; he does not give up his 'brave language, braver deeds' (see the note on 'brave' on pages 54-5) easily, even though he gives them up confidently.

The opposition of the two worlds furnishes much of Herbert's finest poetry. Of those quoted above, *Easter Wings* and *The Collar* are both on the subject of backsliding, the second particularly suggesting the richness of Herbert's former life. Much more explicit, however, is the first of five poems entitled *Affliction*.

Here Herbert is using no particular 'device'; the poem is a direct and gripping narrative in a straightforward stanza-form. Its statements are startlingly bold. 'When first thou didst entice to me thy heart . . .' The implications of 'entice' have an impudence which reminds one of Donne addressing a mistress, not a clergyman addressing God. Again:

Whereas my birth and spirit rather took
    The way that takes the town,
Thou didst *betray* me to a ling'ring book . . .

The conclusion is stranger still:

> Well, I will change the service, and go seek
>   Some other master out.
> Ah, my dear God, though I am clean forgot,
> Let me not love thee, if I love thee not.

The last line, in its uncompromising paradox, is one of the boldest in all Metaphysical poetry. What does it mean? One interpretation is: 'Let me not be a priest at all, if I can't sincerely like it.' But it is more probable that the last couplet is another Herbert *volte-face*, such as we have seen above at the end of *The Collar* and occurs also at the end of the second *Jordan* poem. The poet repents, and—knowing how deep a pleasure and fulfilment he gets from loving God—says: 'I don't deserve to love you, if I don't now love you in spite of all my affliction.'

This difficulty is most unusual in Herbert, and makes the poem seem—as indeed its subject-matter also suggests—a particularly personal one: a private communication with God. Its fierceness and honesty, with the puzzling conclusion, make it nevertheless a most disturbing poem for any reader.

The Pearl, although a sober and calm poem, has again a particularly personal ring; significantly, it is again on the subject of the fine things Herbert has renounced. One of the splendid qualities of Herbert's humility is its freedom from false modesty; and this poem is an impressive and manly claim to have mastered or come to know well 'the ways . . . of Learning . . . of Honour . . . of Pleasure'—a claim which makes the more pointed the renunciation of them at the end:

> I know all these, and have them in my hand:
> Therefore not seeled, but with open eyes
> I fly to Thee, and fully understand
> Both the main sale and the commodities . . .

—that is, I'm submitting myself to you with my eyes open; I've read all the small print in the agreement (*seeled = eyes sewn up*, from hawking).

For those who see Herbert as a figure so saintly as to be

untroubled by physical desires and emotions, the *Pleasure* verse is a feeling rebuke:

> I know the ways of Pleasure . . .
> The propositions of hot blood and brains . . .
> My stuff is flesh, not brass; my senses live,
> And grumble oft . . .

Two other poems on this question must be mentioned: *Frailty* and *The Forerunners*—two of the most moving Metaphysical poems, though there is no sound and fury about them, as with much of Donne, nor dazzling imagery as in the later Metaphysicals.

Frailty might well be contrasted with Donne's *Batter my heart*; basically they make the same plea, that God shall help the poet in his unequal struggle against temptation. The form Herbert's poem takes is characteristically different from the thunder of Donne's. The diction is wistful. The first stanza scorns

> What upon trust
> Is Styled honour, riches, or fair eyes
> But is fair dust!

(The rhyme here, coming upon Herbert's most expressive image, has a force of contempt.) But the second voices a wavering:

> But when I view abroad both regiments,
> The world's and Thine—
> Thine clad with simpleness and sad events;
> The other fine,
> Full of glory and gay weeds,
> Brave language, braver deeds—
> That which was dust before doth quickly rise,
> And prick mine eyes.

Notice the precision and appropriateness of the last image. It was dust in the first stanza; now, as dust does when it rises to trouble us, it hurts his eyes and makes tears start. The neatness and pathos of this is supported by the nimble assonance of 'quickly rise' and 'prick mine eyes'.

The last stanza confesses insecurity and pleads for aid:

> O brook not this, lest if what even now
> > My foot did tread
> > ... may a Babel prove,
> Commodious to conquer heaven and Thee,
> > Planted in me.

This is one of the few 'unresolved' poems in *The Temple*. *The Fore-runners*, on the other hand, is superbly resolved; linked with the smaller poem *Life*, it expresses with a ring of truth Herbert's attitude towards the death which his frail health suggested might come early. White hairs in the poet's head are compared to the chalk-marks which the fore-runners who were requisitioning rooms would make when a King was coming—the King, in this case, being God. If his poetic abilities leave him, he cares not ('I pass not'), provided he is still able to find the words 'Thou art still my God'.

In a powerful middle section, the poet regrets that the fine language and ideas of poetry should be wasted on secular subjects; the following epigram has a grand, Keatsian or even Shakespearean, movement rare in Herbert's restrained poetry:

> True Beauty dwells on high; ours is a flame
> > But borrow'd thence to light us thither;
> Beauty and beauteous words should go together.

And in the final stanza the poet returns to his confidence, in lines again noticeable for their dignity and nobility:

> Go, birds of Spring; let Winter have his fee;
> > Let a bleak paleness chalk the door,
> So all within be livelier than before.

Variety

Herbert's works are, of course, less voluminous than those of Donne, and range less widely. It is a disturbing thought that the very qualities which are so admirable in Herbert are also those which seem to limit him, by comparison with Donne. The fluctuations of Donne's emotion and belief, the fierceness and tension of his verse, are attributes Herbert must have sought to avoid; yet they are part of Donne's special appeal to us, and contribute to the span of his poetry.

This must be recognised. It must not, however, be allowed to distort our evaluation of Herbert, who is one of the best English poets in most things, and the best of all in some things. His work may not offer the terrific tension, nor the variety, we find in Donne; but tension and variety are there. Slowly but with a sure life of their own the poems enact dramas of much profundity; a man who could write *The Collar* or *Conscience* ('Peace, prattler, do not lour') was not lacking in vigour. As for variety, we must remember that *The Temple* was put together as a book designed to help its readers towards peace-of-mind and salvation; Herbert did not, obviously, include in it poems of despair or doubt, and it is possible that he wrote some. One such, indeed, we have— *Perseverance*—which almost anticipates G. M. Hopkins in its last lines:

> Only my soul hangs on Thy promises,
> With face and hands clinging unto Thy breast;
> Clinging and crying, crying without cease,
>   'Thou art my Rock, thou art my Rest.'

Within *The Temple*, there is a far greater variety than this short chapter has been able to indicate, from the intricate meditations of *The Sacrifice* (a great though little-read poem) to the colloquialisms of *The Quip*:

> Then came brave Glory puffing by
> In silks that whistled, who but he!

—or the measured majesty of *Mortification* (yet another of the fine device-poems: the third line of each stanza ends with the word 'breath', the last line with 'Death', the subject of the poem being this progression, which is mirrored in each stanza by these repetitions).

Perhaps the most extraordinary poem in *The Temple* is *Prayer*, a sonnet of phrases without a verb, an impressionist evocation of something the poet valued most highly. The shorthand method enables the poet to draw together an astonishing number of images, from the bigness of:

> The Christian plummet sounding heav'n and earth

—to the almost Romantic, emotional vagueness of the last couplet:

> Church-bells beyond the stars heard, the soul's blood,
> The land of spices, something understood.

This, like much of Herbert's best, is entirely original. That 'something understood' must wait until the nineteenth or twentieth century to find even a distant relation.

CONCLUSION

The Temple was a best-seller when first published. Since then, Herbert has never ceased to be praised, but often for the wrong reasons (piety is not really a literary merit) or in ways which disguised his real importance. Probably he will never appeal to so wide an audience as Donne, who offers a more sensational and varied talent, and who pleases agnostic and believer alike. Many of Herbert's most appreciative readers do not share his religious beliefs, but there are always others who cannot or will not read Herbert because of what amounts to religious prejudice.

It must be admitted that most devotional poetry tends to be sanctimonious and dull. Herbert's achievement is the more notable: that from so calm and confident a heart, from so orthodox a religious position, he could write poetry which so completely avoids tedium, predictability and insincerity. Perhaps the reason is that his poems are mostly private, written not firstly for preaching purposes, though he was content to think that they might work that way also, but as conversations with God, where—to a man of his intelligence—there was no temptation to humbug. We can understand why Gerard Manley Hopkins found Herbert his 'strongest tie to the English Church', for Hopkins's own religious poetry is private. And it should be for us the most humbling realisation of all that the imagination, the Wit, the complexity of Herbert's poems—which satisfy so fully what the secular world expects of poetry—were written without the poet's wishing, or during his lifetime allowing, for publication, or the admiration of any man.

8

Vaughan, Marvell, Crashaw and others

HENRY VAUGHAN

Vaughan was born in 1621 in Brecknockshire, and lived in the region for most of his life, except his student years. He and his twin-brother Thomas were educated at Oxford; Thomas became a philosopher of note, Henry left Oxford without a degree, studied law in London, and presumably studied medicine also, since he later practised as a doctor in Wales. He died in 1695.

His early poetry, which goes unread today, was Platonic love-poetry in the style of Donne. Round about 1648 Vaughan underwent some kind of religious conversion. Possible causes of this were illness, the fact that Vaughan fought on the losing, Royalist side in the Civil War, and perhaps also the deaths of friends or relations. In literary and devotional terms, however, the converting influence was George Herbert's poetry, as Vaughan himself said, and as his own work shows. Vaughan's major poetry—all devotional—appeared in *Silex Scintillans* (1650-55: he was still, therefore, a young man). The remainder of his life was passed in Wales, in comparative obscurity.

'There is no example in English literature,' says F. E. Hutchinson, Vaughan's biographer, 'of one poet borrowing so extensively from another.' Herbert, of course, had died when Vaughan was only twelve; but his poetry was still widely read, and in Vaughan we have an extraordinary case of a poet whose highest aim was to do as well as Herbert, even in Herbert's own manner. Usually when a poet—or any artist—models his style on that of another, he does not achieve the highest effects: his work *reads* like an imitation. And when very closely following Herbert, Vaughan is perhaps not at his very best. But in general, Vaughan's poetry is amazing for its distinctive and personal skills; it offers qualities found in no other pre-Romantic poet.

About the influence of Herbert, Vaughan himself wrote, in a Latin poem translated here by Edmund Blunden:

> then I went
> To learned Herbert's kind encouragement,
> Herbert, the pride of our Latinity;
> Six years with double gifts he guided me,
> Method and love, and mind and heart conspired ...

The last line is a superb account of Herbert's excellence, and, to some extent, of Metaphysical poetry in general.

Vaughan's poetry *looks* like Herbert's on the page: there are many varieties of stanza and rhyme, with only one frequently-used form—the tetrameter (eight-syllable) couplet, which was fashionable (it seems) in Vaughan's day and not in Herbert's. Vaughan's titles repeatedly echo Herbert's, and even announce poems on similar themes to the respective Herbert poems. The stanza-form of Vaughan's *The Star* is very similar to that of Herbert's poem of the same name, and most other of Vaughan's titles are in the Herbert manner, as is the poet's verse and diction. (The imagery, however, as Chapter 5 said, shows no particular resemblance.)

One of Vaughan's greatest poems, *The World*, ends with the same device which ends Herbert's *Jordan, II* and *The Collar*— the whispered voice of God or wisdom. Where Herbert has:

> But as I rav'd and grew more fierce and wild
>   At every word,
> Methoughts I heard one calling, *Child!*
>   And I replied, *My Lord.*

THE COLLAR

Vaughan writes:

> But as I did their madness so discuss
>   One whisper'd thus,
> *This Ring the Bride-groom did for none provide*
>   *But for his Bride.*

The echo is unmistakable; yet the Vaughan has—particularly when read in context—its own force, and does not suffer by being laid alongside the Herbert.

Those interested in Vaughan must read Herbert (and Chapter 7 of this book): most of the superficial characteristics of Vaughan's work are learnt from Herbert (to mention one other, the 'patterning' of poems, as in the first dozen lines of Vaughan's *The Water-Fall*). In more important ways, however, Vaughan is completely original; he offers something very different from Herbert.

Ease

Firstly, Vaughan is a lighter and less intellectual poet than Herbert, let alone Donne. This, like other differences, is partly a matter of a change in the style of poetry through the seventeenth century: the mid-century, when Vaughan was writing, produced in general a calmer diction, an easier and more song-like verse, and statements of greater clarity (though usually of less profundity) than the time of Shakespeare, Donne and Jonson. (Milton is a tremendous exception to this generalisation, as he is to most generalisations.)

The reader who is interested in following up this point might read, in addition to the poets discussed in this chapter, some lyrics of Richard Lovelace, Edmund Waller, Sir John Suckling and other popular poets of the mid-century. English poetry was settling down, controlling and polishing itself, after the explosive developments in diction and verse-rhythm of Elizabethan and Jacobean poetry. In the eighteenth century, poetry prided itself upon discipline and smoothness; and although it is also poetry heavy with thought and seriousness, it developed from an intermediate period of comparative frivolity. Abraham Cowley, the most popular Metaphysical poet in the later years of the century, shows this change very clearly. His poetry is often upon serious subjects, and bedecked with rather grotesque conceits; but it lacks the real tussling of ideas and language which one meets in Donne and Herbert, and as a result the verse is rather dully regular and the images can seem unnecessary. Cowley's elegy

On the Death of Mr Crashaw (1656) is written in Heroic couplets (iambic pentameter couplets)—the same form as Donne's *Satires* and Carew's *Elegy on the Death of Dr Donne*, but handled very differently. Cowley's couplets are units, like those of Pope fifty years later; there is enjambement, but it is always mild and easy to accept. Also in 1656 Cowley published the following lines:

> The busy Sun (and one would guess
> By's drunken fiery face no less)
> Drinks up the Sea, and when he's done,
> The Moon and Stars drink up the Sun.
> They drink and dance by their own light,
> They drink and revel all the night.
> Nothing in Nature's sober found,
> But an eternal Health goes round.
> Fill up the Bowl, then, fill it high,
> Fill all the Glasses there, for why
> Should every creature drink but I,
> Why, Man of Morals, tell me why?

The comparative obviousness of the verse here (leaving aside the vulgarity of the ideas) is a mark not only of Cowley but of the tendency of the time. It is interesting to see how Vaughan, Crashaw and Marvell seem to have taken over something of the lightness and ease of their contemporaries without sacrificing subtlety. The ease shows most in tetrameter couplets; but it is also a matter of diction, as these lines from Vaughan's *The Morning-Watch* show:

> All the long hours
> Of night, and Rest
> Through the still shrouds
> Of Sleep, and Clouds,
> This Dew fell on my Breast;
> O how it bloods,
> And spirits all my Earth!

Donne and Herbert tend always towards simplicity—but also towards a certain austerity; of this there is very little in Vaughan, who *enjoys* life, and is not afraid to say so in the gayest or most

128

child-like ways. This point will be incidentally developed in the course of the following paragraphs.

Drama

D. J. Enright has suggested that Vaughan 'lacks a sense of climax', and it is indeed true that his poems do not have the unmistakable shape and structure of Herbert's. When Enright says, however, that Vaughan is 'noticeably less dramatic than Herbert', he may be misleading. Vaughan is an excitable poet: his openings are more frequently dramatic than those of Herbert:

> They are all gone into the world of light!
>   And I alone sit lingering here.
>
> (Untitled poem)

> O Joys! Infinite Sweetness! With what flowers
> And shoots of glory, my soul breaks, and buds!
>
> THE MORNING-WATCH

> Ah! what time wilt thou come?
>
> THE DAWNING

> Come, come, what do I here?
>
> (Untitled poem)

> 'Twas so, I saw thy birth
>
> THE SHOWER

—and, supremely:

> Silence, and stealth of days! 'tis now
>   Since thou art gone
> Twelve hundred hours . . .
>
> (Untitled poem)

Exclamation marks are very frequent in Vaughan's first lines.
  But the really dramatic quality of Vaughan is his flashing mystical vision, the moments of utter surprise for the reader when something completely new suddenly breaks across the poem. The excitement it offers is far from rational; the drama is in the extremely clear presentation of the dazzling images. Vaughan's boldest statements are phrased in his 'easiest', most

direct syntax, and the effect is to rule out any possibility of compromise or doubt. (Much of Blake's simple poetry works in a similar way.)

Life is a fix'd, discerning light . . .

QUICKNESS

I see them walking in an air of glory

THEY ARE ALL GONE . . .

Prayer is
The world in tune . . .

THE MORNING-WATCH

The most striking example of this is the opening of *The World*:

I saw Eternity the other night

Here the phrase 'the other night' belongs clearly to colloquial language. The whole opening is almost embarrassing: we are listening, we feel, either to a seer or to an idiot.

This is all part of the child-like quality often noticed in Vaughan, which he seems at times to cultivate, since it is appropriate to his belief. Not only is his attitude to God one of the most trusting humility, accompanied by continual fits of sheer delight at the idea of God; but he believes that in childhood man is pure and good in ways it is almost impossible for him to maintain as he grows older.

Childhood as Innocence

Vaughan's attitude to childhood was an unusual one for his time, though it finds something of a parallel in the poems and prose of his contemporary, Thomas Traherne. (Traherne is not Metaphysical in character, and cannot be discussed in this book; but he is a genuine and satisfying poet and an even finer prose writer, who does resemble Vaughan in the simplicity and whiteness and happiness of his work.) Both poets see divine innocence in the life of childhood, but with Traherne there is less antithesis between this and the life of adulthood. Vaughan, in *The Retreat* and *Childhood*, seems almost to anticipate the eighteenth-century French thinker, Jean-Jacques Rousseau, who believed that a child was best left to grow according to his instincts. ('As God made them,' Rousseau wrote, 'all things are good; as man touches them, so they degenerate.' We should 'let childhood mature in the child'.)

More striking is the closeness with which Vaughan seems to anticipate Wordsworth. The famous *Ode on Intimations of Immortality From Recollections of Early Childhood* follows Vaughan to the extent that one wonders if Wordsworth knew the earlier poet's work; though this is unlikely to have been the case.

Here is Wordsworth:

> Not in entire forgetfulness,
> And not in utter nakedness,
> But trailing clouds of glory do we come
> From God, who is our home . . .
> . . . though inland far we be,
> Our Souls have sight of that immortal sea
> Which brought us hither.

—and here Vaughan:

> When yet I had not walk'd above
> A mile, or two, from my first love,
> And looking back (at that short space)
> Could see a glimpse of his bright face;
> When on some gilded Cloud, or flower
> My gazing soul would dwell an hour,
> And in those weaker glories spy
> Some shadows of eternity;

THE RETREAT

Childhood develops the subject much more explicitly: childhood, says Vaughan, is the state of innocence, and maturity is corrupting.

> Since all that age doth teach is ill,
> Why should I not love childhood still?
> Why, if I see a rock or shelf
> Shall I from thence cast down myself?
> Or by complying with the world,
> From the same precipice be hurl'd?

Childhood is the state which Vaughan studies and scans 'more than e'er I studied man'. If it were possible to be still a child, he would quickly choose it:

> And by mere playing go to Heaven.

But the poem opens with the admission that this cannot be:

> I cannot reach it; and my striving eye
> Dazzles at it, as at eternity.

—another dramatic opening, again using Vaughan's favourite imagery.

This poem makes an important comment on Vaughan. He is not really like a nineteenth-century Romantic poet: the developments of Wordsworth's *Immortality Ode* and Vaughan's *Retreat* after this early coincidence are different, and in keeping with their periods. Vaughan's poem laments the baseness of earthly life, as religious men of his age did, whereas Wordsworth's poem celebrates earthly life. And Vaughan might well have been horrified at the teachings of Rousseau or of Blake. Yet the uniqueness of Vaughan can best be described by the reference to Romanticism. He is a Metaphysical poet who reminds us at times of a much later age. His subject-matter is that which is *evoked* rather than identified and argued over; and whereas Metaphysical poetry always links reason and emotion, and puts up a logical front, there are times in Vaughan where logic is far off, and we are presented not with meditation but with vision or intuition, unexplained and inexplicable.

'Times', 'moments', 'images': these are the words in which Vaughan's greatness tends to be described. The superb moments of Vaughan quoted in this chapter (and others) are, in their way, unbeatable in English poetry; yet few would deny that as a poet he is finally inferior to Donne and Herbert and possibly to Marvell also. The reason must be his relative inability to *sustain* an excellence through a poem, or to construct in perfect proportion. It is often remarked that very few of Vaughan's poems are quite the right length. Again, whereas part of the strength of Metaphysical poetry is its ability to tease the reader and yet suggest that the writer himself knows exactly where he is going, with Vaughan one is not always sure that the poet himself knows how the poem will end. It is not impossible to imagine the stanzas of *Quickness* being re-arranged, and the new reader not noticing.

Nor is Vaughan's excellence so consistent or pervasive as that of Donne or that of Herbert. Donne is hardly ever merely competent and traditional; in Herbert one can always admire the craftsmanship of verse and rhythm, even where the thought is unexciting. Vaughan read in quantity is less rewarding, and the fine moments occur amidst expanses of more or less routine verse.

It follows that Vaughan's most successful poems are those which combine the poet's unique vision with a carefully-planned and worked-out structure (such as *The World*) or which are limited and controlled to a length appropriate to the idea (such as *The Retreat, Peace,* or *Silence, and stealth of days!*). *The Retreat*, in the same couplet-form as Marvell's *To His Coy Mistress*, shares the neatness and conciseness of that poem, as well as its imaginative power. The couplets move briskly but not hurriedly; there are two clear paragraphs, just the right length for what they are saying, and the verse enacts the sense in a similar way (see page 47).

The Shower is a less ambitious poem, equally excellent in its proportions: it resembles in structure some of Herbert's shorter lyrics such as *Life*, though the partially-frustrated idea ('my hard heart, that's bound up, and asleep') would not be treated in the present tense by Herbert. The conclusion shows again Vaughan's liking for the colloquial child's tone, when he could assume it:

> Perhaps at last
> (Some such showers past)
> My God would give a sun-shine after rain.

An incidental habit of Vaughan's which links with this naïve tone is his use of alliteration. This device is not in itself a sign of naïvety, of course; but the way Vaughan uses it is very direct and unsophisticated. Donne or Herbert would probably have scorned as jingle these lines from *The Retreat*:

Before I taught my tongue to wound
My conscience with a sinful sound
Or had the black art to dispense
A several sin to every sense . . .
. . . O how I long to travel back
And tread again that ancient track!

To modern readers it tends to be rather pleasing: it is, after all, part of a clear and confident statement which it helps to support. Indeed, Vaughan almost always uses this device to link words which need linking, and often his most expressive condensed descriptions result:

I straight perceiv'd my spring
Mere stage, and show,
My walk a monstrous, mountain'd thing
Rough-cast with rocks, and snow . . .

REGENERATION

False life! a foil and no more, when
Wilt thou be gone?
Thou foul deception of all men
That would not have the true come on.

. . . Thou art a toilsome Mole, or less
A moving mist
But life is, what none can express,
A quickness, which my God hath kissed.

QUICKNESS

Perhaps Vaughan's finest poem is *The World*. This consists of four long and intricate stanzas of a vaguely allegorical kind: the first describes the Lover, wasting his 'dear Treasure' of love and loyalty 'upon a flower'; the second stingingly describes the Statesman:

It rain'd about him blood and tears, but he
Drank them as free . . .

—the third shows the miser 'on a heap of rust' and the Epicure who 'placed heaven in sense' (that is, maintained that the only heaven was in physical sensation); and the fourth describes a few

134

'who soared up into the Ring'. The Ring is presented in the first lines of the poem, some of the most majestic in our language:

> I saw Eternity the other night
> Like a great Ring of pure and endless light,
>   All calm, as it was bright,
> And round beneath it, Time in hours, days, years
>   Driv'n by the spheres
> Like a vast shadow mov'd, in which the world
>   And all her train were hurl'd;

However much we admire poetic virtuosity—'strong lines' as the Elizabethans called it; every rift 'loaded with ore' as Keats advised—the greatest passages of all poetry are when this too is transcended, and the simplest, most genuine language is used. This is a matter of opinion, and readers have their own preferences. Matthew Arnold found Wordsworth's 'And never lifted up a single stone' to be, *in its context*, sublime; in Shakespeare one might choose King Lear's:

> Pray, do not mock me:
> I am a very foolish fond old man;

5, 7, 59-60

—or Hamlet's 'To be or not to be, that is the question'; or Cleopatra's:

> Peace, peace!
> Dost thou not see my baby at my breast,
> That sucks the nurse asleep?

Metaphysical poetry has many examples of this ultimate simplicity. Donne's: 'She's all States, and all Princes, I, Nothing else is'; the whole of Herbert's *Love*; Marvell's 'green thought in a green shade'; and all the finest bits of Vaughan, quoted above. The opening to *The World* is exceptional in the perfect coincidence of verse and meaning; after the shortish and challenging first line, a second which 'draws out' the Ring, followed by the great pause of the third line: 'All calm' (two successive stresses, followed by comma and caesura) 'as it was bright'; the repeated rhyme-sound confirming the certainty of the vision and the perfection of the Ring.

This Vaughan could hardly sustain. Most of the poem is in fact a sound, diligent development of the vision, and even the last stanza, which returns to the Ring, cannot recapture all the power of the original statement. The poem concludes, in fact, with a conceit one can barely tolerate:

> *This Ring the Bride-groom did for none provide*
> *But for his Bride.*

Once the Ring has been so vividly presented as a huge structure spanning the universe, the attempt to introduce a Brobdingnagian finger into it is really grotesque: a suspension of the pictorial imagination is necessary. *The World* hardly justifies its own opening; but then there is no grander opening anywhere.

ANDREW MARVELL

Marvell was born in 1618 in Hull, the son of a Calvinist priest, and educated in Hull and at Cambridge. He then worked as a tutor, and travelled abroad. His lyric poetry was probably written mainly during these years, his twenties and thirties. Although he had seemed inclined to the Royalist side, he eventually became a fervent follower of Cromwell and a friend of John Milton; he was Member of Parliament for Hull from 1659 till his death in 1678. He continued to write poetry, but it is his earlier lyrics which are remembered and studied today, and his reputation rests on comparatively few poems.

In Marvell, the influence of Ben Jonson and the Cavalier Poets is superficially more apparent than that of Donne. Marvell's verse moves in regular, graceful lines, with many classical references and wit-devices such as paradox. Whereas there was a close personal and family tie between Donne and Herbert, and an acknowledged indebtedness of Vaughan to Herbert, Marvell has no direct descent from any of these. Yet in what he actually chooses to say, and in the tone adopted as well as in his imagery, Marvell is fundamentally Metaphysical.

Like Vaughan (and each of the major Metaphysicals), Marvell is a very distinctive poet with his own manner. What is more, although we may read fewer poems by Marvell, his range even in those poems is wider than Vaughan's, and the development of each poem better carried through. There is no single pervading image or subject like that of death in Donne or light in Vaughan. If anything emerges as especially Marvellian, it is an exceptional sensitivity to the physical world, as organised in poetry. He is not a free-ranging Romantic; nature to him is *The Garden*, rich and beautiful but trimmed and disciplined (and, in the poem, ornamented with classical references and metaphysical fancies).

Nevertheless, in places Marvell creates the most vivid sense-impressions of anyone between Shakespeare and Keats:

> Ripe apples drop about my head;
> The luscious Clusters of the vine
> Upon my mouth do crush their Wine;

THE GARDEN

Notice the 'p' sounds in the first line, describing the plop of apples to the ground; and the indulgence of 'l' and 'u' in 'luscious Clusters' and 'crush'. One is meant to savour the words, like the fruit. This passage may have been remembered by Gerard Manley Hopkins when writing his famous lines:

> How a lush-kept plush-capped sloe
> Will, mouthed to flesh-burst,
> Gush! flush the man, the being, with it . . .

Hopkins knew Marvell's work and described it as 'most rich and nervous'. The 'nervous' here is a superb perception: it suggests not only this vivid sense-awareness but also a quality of tension, almost of suffering, which underlies most of Marvell's work.

This statement at once needs explanation and qualification. Far more than Donne, more even than Herbert, Marvell restrains his emotions. The comparative regularity of his verse assures that, and so does the frequency of precise Latinate diction. Reading Marvell, one is conscious as much of his sense of humour as of any sadness. His most famous poem, *To His Coy Mistress*, is full of jokes, from the bathos of:

> Thou by the Indian *Ganges* side
> Shouldst rubies find: I by the Tide
> Of Humber would complain . . .

(Even in Marvell's day the Humber must have seemed a particularly unexotic estuary.)
—to the 'cheek' of making the sun run, in the last line.

In *The Garden*, Marvell suggests that the apparent amorous passions of the Gods are really a worship of greenery, which in this poem, in deliberate provocation, Marvell is affecting to prefer:

> Apollo hunted Daphne so,
> Only that she might laurel grow.

(In the story Daphne did indeed become laurel as Apollo hunted her, but Apollo was considerably frustrated by the evasion.)

In a later stanza the poet mischievously says that:

> Two Paradises 'twere in one
> To live in Paradise alone.

Yet can we completely ignore the hint of the tart bachelor in these last lines? There is more than a possibility of distress here, and perhaps in the whole poem, urbane and good-natured though it is:

> Fair Quiet, have I found thee here,
> And Innocence thy Sister dear!
> Mistaken long, I sought you then
> In busy Companies of Men.

Many readers have felt the genuine anguish (finely controlled though it is) in the middle section of *To His Coy Mistress* ('But at my back I always hear . . .'). And in the last section of that poem it is worth noting the violence, a touch of desperation, beginning in such words as 'devour', 'sport' and 'slow-chapp'd power', and emerging fully in:

Let us roll all our Strength, and all
Our Sweetness, up into one Ball:
And tear our Pleasures, with rough strife,
Thorough the Iron gates of Life.

This is a savage image: the suggestions it may have for us of cinematic orgies or motor-bikes are for once not wholly inappropriate. The tone is similar to Antony's 'Let's have one other gaudy night' in *Antony and Cleopatra* or to Faustus's attempt to hide from his horror in the arms of Helen: and both these heroes are already doomed. Of course the poem does not mean to allow for such sombre moralising: it is a traditional *Carpe Diem* poem (see page 27) and the energy of life and of sexual desire drives it; but the chariot of death is certainly audible, and the lines are underlain with a tension that implies pain. In this respect, Marvell partially resembles Donne.

As for *The Definition of Love* (see pages 65-7), although the abstract form chosen—a 'definition' where the beloved never appears—might seem to indicate indifference, and a quick glance at the poem might suggest comparative triviality, it is a poem of most painful suggestiveness. It is of course, like *To His Coy Mistress*, an artifice: it may have been written for, or about, no actual love; but it is no less personal for that. The violence of this poem is an aspect of Marvell's mind, and one which has had less attention than his well-known wit and grace.

There are other examples. In the otherwise gentle *Picture of little T.C.* one meets this image of 'conquering eyes':

with their glancing wheels, they drive
In Triumphs over Hearts that strive ...

(Note the pun on 'glancing'.) This is an image of physical suffering which echoes the fixing of the 'extended Soul' and the driving of Fate's 'iron wedges' in *The Definition of Love*. In *The Fair Singer*, the lover's art 'can wreath My fetters of the very Air I breathe'. In *The Coronet*, Marvell echoes Donne momentarily in asking God to 'shatter ... my curious frame'. And the *Dialogue between the Soul and the Body* is, because of the conceit which it develops (that the Soul is enslaved by the body, and the body by the Soul), a catalogue of tortures.

One may notice also how many of Marvell's major poems deal with subjects of frustration or grief (*Eyes and Tears*, *The Coronet*, the *Dialogues* between *Pleasure* and *Soul* and between *Soul* and *Body*, *The Nymph Complaining for the Death of Her Faun*, *The Definition of Love* and several others). This is not the whole story: this poet's complexity of mood goes with a considerable range of emotion. As well as painful tension, there is in Marvell a visionary happiness at moments, similar to that of Vaughan but characterised more by 'colour' than by 'light'. Such poems are *The Bermudas*, *The Garden* and *On a Drop of Dew*. In each case there is exceptional vividness of physical sensation.

An example (already quoted earlier in this book) from the *Dialogue between the Soul and the Body*, the first ten lines, will illustrate again this disturbing vividness, even in grotesque fantasy, and also an entirely different quality of Marvell which needs attention—his intellectual cleverness.

> SOUL: O who shall, from this Dungeon, raise
> A Soul enslav'd so many ways?
> With bolts of Bones, that fetter'd stands
> In Feet; and manacl'd in Hands.
> Here blinded with an Eye; and there
> Deaf with the drumming of an Ear.
> A Soul hung up, as 'twere, in Chains
> Of Nerves, and Arteries, and Veins.
> Tortur'd, besides each other part.
> In a vain Head, and double Heart.

Marvell was a scholar, and a poet of wit; and these lines offer us many incidental subtleties of a witty kind. The third and fourth lines offer word-play, beginning with assonance in 'bolts of Bones', proceeding through the near-pun of 'fetter'd' and 'feet' (both words come from the Latin 'pes, pedis', a foot), to the disguised pun of 'manacl'd in Hands' (Latin 'manus', a hand). The fifth and sixth lines develop the conceit into paradox —'blinded with an Eye' and 'Deaf with the drumming of an Ear': this is not perversity, but an expression of a common religious theme, that physical sensations may distract from spiritual experience. To the Soul, the eye and the ear really are obstacles, because they look at and listen to profane things. The next two lines recall not only surrealist painting (see page 82) but also anatomy-drawings of veins, arteries and the nervous system, which seem like the chains in which a criminal was hung for torture or execution.

There is much of this intricacy in Marvell—more than in any other Metaphysical poet except, occasionally, Herbert. Latin lurks behind many of Marvell's lines; as William Empson points out, there is a hidden Latin pun on the famous description of Charles I's execution:

> He nothing common did or mean
> Upon that memorable scene;
> But with his keener eye
> The Axe's edge did try.

HORATIAN ODE

Acies in Latin (the word Axe suggests it) meant both 'eyesight' and 'sharp edge'. This offers to a scholar a delight similar to that felt when a clever crossword clue is solved; and yet the ordinary reader who misses the pun still gathers the main force of the lines, and is not excluded from pleasure because of his lack of Latin.

Most of these subtleties you (and I) of course miss, unless they are pointed out for us by editors or commentators. But, where they are pointed out, it is worth while following them up in the text; and in general we should not underestimate Marvell's intellectual strength, just because it presents itself in comparatively simple diction and apparently naïve picture-drawing. The most important poem where one can miss a lot is *The Garden*, in particular the two celebrated verses, the quiet climax of the poem, where the Mind 'Withdraws into its happiness' while the Soul 'into the boughs does glide'.

RICHARD CRASHAW

Crashaw was born in 1612, the son of a Puritan preacher; and educated at Cambridge, where in 1635 he became a Fellow of

Peterhouse, and where he became associated with High-Church-men. Later, probably to avoid Puritan restrictions, he left England, and lived in Paris and later in Rome and Loreto. On the Continent he became a Roman Catholic, and was closely associated with the Roman Church, though we do not know whether he actually took orders. He died abroad in 1649. *Steps to the Temple* was published in 1646 (after he had left England) and *Carmen Deo Nostro*, the final edition of his poems, in Paris in 1652.

Crashaw presents special problems to a modern reader. His poetry is not so difficult to understand as that of Donne or even of Marvell; but many readers find themselves out of sympathy with it. It has been suggested, convincingly, that this is because he inclines towards Continental, and particularly Italian, modes of poetry and religious thought, rather than towards English. The conceits of Italian poetry were far more outrageous than anything any English poet perpetrated; and Crashaw's conceits, influenced almost certainly by Italian poetry, seem too extreme for some English readers. Italian churches are brightly painted, with bejewelled altars, English churches predominantly of stark stone; the difference is everywhere evident in the hot colour of Crashaw's ornamentation.

Crashaw's poetry is extremely artificial, much more so than most, and it can seem to lack an onward force, as it lingers over its devices. In a good baroque architecture, or music, the orna-mentation decorates a strong fundamental structure; Crashaw's poems too often seem all surface, all glitter—one loses the sense of where the poet is going. In Chapter 5 it was suggested that Crashaw often becomes engrossed in the material of his images, not in what they are supposed to be depicting.

The best of Crashaw's poems escape this charge, more or less; the urgency to say something is there; and a few of these will be discussed in a moment. His best, even so, is restless; the un-ceasing images of love, violent sensation, and pain—the word 'blushing' may be taken both to represent and to summarise them—constantly titillate, but never grow towards a climax, or even a direction. The sense of the poem may be clear and lively;

142

the erotic imagery, beautiful and disturbing in its way, tends to fuzz up the picture and to be interchangeable from poem to poem.

But he is a poet about whom there is much disagreement. C. V. Wedgwood wrote, as recently as 1950, that he was 'by far the greatest of the metaphysical poets after Donne'; and perhaps few people would deny the excellence of Crashaw's finer passages and poems. Certainly he is a poet standing very much on his own in English poetry, in strength and weakness.

It is strange to think that Crashaw's father was a Puritan; his son could hardly have been more differently inclined. There is a feminine element in him completely foreign to Puritanism, and indeed to such a poet as Herbert (to whom the title *Steps to the Temple* just *may* be a tribute); it shows itself in the tenderness which is Crashaw's finest quality, and links him to the Roman Church in which the Virgin Mary and many women saints occupy such important positions (Crashaw's most celebrated poems are, perhaps, the *Hymn to St Teresa*, the *Letter to the Countess of Denbigh* and *The Weeper*, on the subject of Mary Magdalen's tears). Feminine also is Crashaw's love for perfumes, rich colour and jewels.

More important: Crashaw's poetry, in its ornamented artificiality, repeatedly suggests ritual, and even musical form. Rather than dramatic development, he aims at formal elaboration. This is one reason why Crashaw's poems are so long (as Metaphysical poems go). *The Weeper* develops a question-and-answer approach to a climax only in the last four of its twenty-eight stanzas: all the first twenty-four are very similar to musical variations upon a theme, being in many cases independent of their immediate neighbours, and having each its separate conceit. The *Hymn of the Nativity* develops in the limited and ritualised manner of sung dialogue (a stanza each) between two soloists, with a chorus singing a refrain after each verse and six final stanzas of Full Chorus. Both poems are impressive achievements, but are limited simply by what they set out to do: *The Weeper*, for example, would be a confused and poorer poem if personal emotion, tension or drama were allowed into it, but on the other hand a poem lacking these is severely restricted.

It is still remarkable. A whole poem on tears is a tremendously difficult task for the artist. The first stanza salutes Magdalen's eyes, with metaphor, personification, and paradox:

> Hail, Sister Springs,
> Parents of Silver-footed rills!
> Ever bubbling things!
> Thawing Crystal! Snowy hills!
> Still spending, never spent; I mean
> Thy fair eyes, sweet *Magdalen*.

The second continues this ambitious complexity with the comparison of the eyes to *heavens*, which *sow* stars,

> whose harvest dares
> Promise the earth to countershine
> Whatever makes Heaven's forehead fine.

—personification again; and an extension of the 'shining' metaphor. The third stanza makes a qualifying comment, which disarmingly admits the inaccuracy of one metaphor (the 'harvest' of falling stars suggested) in order to re-assert the star-metaphor. The fourth rather awkwardly describes the tears as being wept 'upwards' and as the 'cream' above the Milky Way—perhaps the first of those conceits in the poem which are liable to worry the reader, and which we can surely accept a few of, when we remember the difficulty of Crashaw's task. And so—or if anything more attractively—the poem continues, through the famous Cherub's breakfast, the Evening's eyes 'red with weeping ... For the Sun that dies', the dew decking the 'primrose's pale cheek', right to the bold conclusion where the tears themselves speak:

> We go not to seek
> The darlings of Aurora's bed,
> The Rose's modest cheek,
> Nor the Violet's humble head.
> ... We go to meet
> A worthy object: Our Lord's feet.

It is easy to sneer at this poem; but rather than that we should respect Crashaw's out-and-out seriousness. Even when using conceits which border on the facetious (the Milky Way and cream, or 'Portable and compendious Oceans'), Crashaw refuses to seek the protection of irony, as other Metaphysicals might do. An ironic tone is often given by less courageous poets to lines or metaphors which they feel to be too naïve or vulnerable; it may prevent the reader from feeling any of the embarrassment we occasionally feel in Crashaw, but may also prevent the simplicity and tenderness we also find in this poet.

This tenderness combines with a more personal tone to make the *Hymn to St Teresa* probably Crashaw's finest poem. Here the poet is not decorating but saying. There are moments of stylised ingenuity, and the pervasive Crashaw love-poetry appears at its most passionate in the strange central section:

> O how oft shalt thou complain
> Of a sweet and subtle pain!
> Of intolerable joys!
> Of a death, in which who dies
> Loves his death, and dies again
> And would for ever be so slain!
> And lives, and dies; and knows not why
> To live; but that he thus may never leave to die.

(See page 56 for a note on the linking of love and death in poetry.)

But here, however ambiguous, there *is* strong emotion, and a forward movement of the short, vigorous lines. The poem's opening, unusually fierce for Crashaw, is well known:

> Love, thou art absolute sole Lord
> Of life and death.

The poem does not maintain this force, but quietens to a simplicity appropriate to the child Teresa:

> She can *love*, and she can *die*.

> . . . Farewell house and farewell home
> She's for the Moors, and Martyrdom.

In this poem one is in no danger of being bored. A similar urge to communicate appears in the *Letter to the Countess of Denbigh*.

The opening superbly depicts the Countess's hesitation: the question is whether to become a Roman Catholic, but typically Crashaw seems to suggest the temptation of a heart in love:

> What Heav'n besieged Heart is this
> Stands Trembling at the Gate of Bliss:
> Holds fast the Door, yet dares not venture
> Fairly to open and to enter?

The whole poem, about ninety lines, continues this eager balance, furthering the effect by the repeated use of alliteration (always frequent in Crashaw, but insistent in almost every line of this poem). The conclusion again unmistakably links God and earthly lover—*To His Coy Mistress* and *Batter my heart . . .* are equally recalled—in lines of pleasing neatness:

> Yield then, O yield, that Love may win
> The Fort at last, and let Life in.
> Yield quickly, lest perhaps you prove
> Death's prey, before the Prize of Love.
> The Fort of your fair Self if 't be not won,
> He is repuls'd indeed, but You're undone.

That, and the humility of *Charitas Nimia: or the Dear Bargain* (though characteristically Crashaw finds room for Cupid even in this, his most Herbert-like poem), are as near as Crashaw comes to personal, direct involvement in his poetry. There is less force here than in the other great Metaphysicals, but there is sufficient to control the whole poem without losing the easy grace which is one of Crashaw's attractions. How many other poems of Crashaw can be accounted successes in this way you must decide (or at least consider) for yourself: the critics have never seemed able to agree.

OTHERS

In a book which has room for only one chapter each on Donne and Herbert, and one shared by Marvell, Vaughan, and Crashaw, her Metaphysical poets must go more or less undiscussed. You would realise, however, that—in so far as it was a recognisable manner—Metaphysical poetry was written by a large number of seventeenth-century poets and would-be poets: it was one of the fashions of its time. The five poets treated above were not the only ones of their time, and most readers would profit from a reading of one of the famous anthologies of Metaphysical poetry (Grierson's, which includes about twenty-five poets, or Helen Gardner's Penguin, which includes thirty-eight and which I have used as a central reference point in writing this book). When the minor practitioners are read, it becomes perhaps more apparent which features are characteristic of the poetic fashion and which are peculiar to the great writers. Mentioned below are a few of the poets which a more comprehensive book on the Metaphysicals might discuss.

William Shakespeare and John Milton are world-famous for their achievements in very different kinds of poetry; but Shakespeare's *Phoenix and the Turtle* and several Milton poems show some Metaphysical qualities. Much more important here is Thomas Carew (1594-1640), whose early career resembled Donne's, but who remained, unlike Donne, in royal service. His poetry, apart from the *Elegy* on Donne, consists mainly of love-poems influenced by Donne and Ben Jonson.

Lord Herbert of Cherbury (1583-1648), George Herbert's brother, was another courtier-poet, writing distinctively Metaphysical poetry of much skill and ingenuity: his most remarkable poem is a sonnet called *Black Beauty*, which has no close parallel in English poetry. The famous and gracious Cavalier lyrics of Richard Lovelace (1618-56) are perhaps faintly Metaphysical in kind.

The two most notorious followers of Donne, both of whom were best-sellers in their time, and who prejudiced Johnson against all Metaphysical poetry (see page 151), are John Cleveland and Abraham Cowley. Cleveland (1613-58), a Royalist imprisoned by Cromwell and later released by Cromwell in respect for his loyalty, imitates the coarseness and ingenuity of Donne without his master's good taste. Without violent crudity

147

and clumsiness, he chatters metaphors so rapidly and indiscriminately that he almost appears to be parodying the style. Cowley (1618-67) is a more important poet. Johnson's age thought him the best of the Metaphysicals, probably because of his increasing smoothness (see pages 127-8), and some of his Hymns and Odes are dignified. His poetry is Donne civilised and cheapened. It is social poetry, glib and rather pleased with itself.

It is an amazing reflection, for our age and all ages, that while the 'literary world' bought and praised Cowley, Cleveland and others—poets almost forgotten less than a hundred years later—Herbert had composed *The Temple* privately at Bemerton, not seeking publication in his lifetime, Vaughan was far from a literary metropolis, in Wales, and Marvell was at most passing an occasional manuscript amongst friends. Donne himself probably received very little real criticism of his poetry. The reactions of an audience—in particular the less favourable reactions—are normally so necessary to an artist if he is to develop; yet those who developed best, who achieved the strongest and most subtly polished work, did so almost in isolation. This is another reminder of the constantly alert and brilliant intelligence of these few men: men for whom only their own best would do.

9
Critical Estimates Over the Years

Texts should always come before criticism, and after it. A critic is only a person like ourselves, though perhaps better trained and more gifted with perception, who approaches a work more or less as we do, and on our behalf. Most criticism is rather boring, and of little use to the general reader or the less experienced student. But you will naturally want to read something of all that has been written on the Metaphysical poets, when you have read the rest of this book and when you have come to know the poets and their work. In any case, the history of critical attitudes to the Metaphysicals is revealing as a story, and tells us something about the poets themselves. So here are some—deliberately brief —notes on the critics; in this chapter I am indebted particularly to Hugh Sykes Davies: *The Poets and Their Critics*, Volume One.

CONTEMPORARY

Jonson was Donne's contemporary, and he represents the attitude of a rival poet, a highly intelligent reader of the classics, and one of those dramatists who captured the vigour and accent of Jacobean life, as Donne captured it in poetry. His critical verdicts—though he probably did not think of them as anything so final—consists of passages from Jonson's *Conversations with William Drummond of Hawthornden* (1619).

'He [Jonson] esteemeth John Done the first poet in the world in some things' and 'affirmeth Done to have written all his best pieces ere he was 25 years old'. The latter statement may mean simply that Jonson had seen little or nothing of Donne's later writing. The former seems canny praise: Donne's was clearly a special kind of poetry, as Jonson's 'in some things' implies.

Less favourably, Jonson is recorded by Drummond as having said: 'That Done, for not keeping of accent, deserved hanging.' Donne's 'roughness' of verse was apparently noted at the time; Jonson's outlook on poetry was professional, and Donne's occasional rule-breaking was bound to incur his disapproval. More serious is the assertion: 'that Done himself, for not being understood, would perish.'

This is a charge which, as the following paragraphs will show, all but came true. Only in this century, when 'difficult' poetry responds better than 'easy' poetry to our methods of approach and our interest, has Metaphysical poetry regained favour. Jonson's criticism tells us that in Donne's own day he was found awkward by many readers; and also that Jonson himself favoured a more easily lyrical, less soul-searching kind of poetry. In his own lifetime Jonson was a poet much admired and imitated, and his influence is perhaps more pervasive in seventeenth-century poetry than that of Donne.

Carew's *Elegy* has been quoted on page 45; other poets, not known well today, also wrote elegies when Donne died, praising him. Walton's *Lives* of Donne and Herbert are warm testimonies of admiration; and the commercial success of Herbert's poetry, coupled with Vaughan's praise, helps to show that these poets were well admired in their own day—or rather, immediately after their deaths, when their poetry was published.

SEVENTEENTH AND EIGHTEENTH CENTURIES

Dryden, the leading poet and critic of Restoration times, was not wholly unappreciative of Donne's work, as the following sentences from *An Essay of Dramatic Poesy*, contrasting Donne and Cleveland, show. The essay is dated 1668.

> . . . we cannot read a verse of Cleveland's without making a face at it, as if every word were a pill to swallow: he gives us many times a hard nut to break our teeth, without a kernel for our pains. So that there is this difference betwixt his *Satires* and doctor Donne's; that the one gives us deep thoughts in common language, though rough cadence; the other gives us common thoughts in abstruse words . . .

Here 'the one' is Donne; 'the other' Cleveland.

But it is Dryden who is responsible for the most famous description of Donne as 'metaphysical', in lines which were long remembered:

> He affects the metaphysics, not only in his satires, but in his amorous verses, where nature only should reign; and perplexes the minds of the fair sex with nice speculations of philosophy, when he should engage their hearts, and entertain them with the softnesses of love.

A DISCOURSE CONCERNING THE ORIGINAL
AND PROGRESS OF SATIRE, 1693

Perhaps the difference of twenty-five years between these two comments to some extent reflects the changing of taste. In the eighteenth century, Donne was to be dismissed by Theobald (the distinguished editor of Shakespeare) as 'nothing but a continued heap of riddles' (1773). Pope preferred Davenant to Donne, but said that Davenant took his 'sententiousness and metaphysics' from Donne. 'Herbert,' Pope said, 'is lower than Crashaw; Sir John Beaumont higher; and Donne a good deal so.' All these remarks are from *Spence's Anecdotes* (1744).

Beside other critics of his time, Samuel Johnson appears almost appreciative of the Metaphysicals. His *Life of Cowley* (1778) contains the first extended criticism of Metaphysical poetry. It is written with Johnson's characteristic clarity and balance—he tries hard to be fair—with his customary generosity of quotation to support his points, always a good sign in a critic. We must realise that he is writing about Cowley, Cleveland and Donne, only one of whom now seems to us a fine poet: on what he says about Cowley and Cleveland he is very largely right.

The accusation, briefly, is that the Metaphysical poets were clever men anxious to show off their cleverness, with little real interest or ability in poetry. There is no freshness of thought or accuracy of description, nor are their words chosen carefully. Johnson notes the specifically Metaphysical characteristic: 'a combination of dissimilar images, or discovery of occult resemblances in things apparently unlike'. (The word 'occult' here is meant to be derogatory, but it hints at the indefinable mystical effect which Metaphysical poetry can achieve in its conceits.) They were self-centred and insensitive:

> ... their courtship was void of fondness and their lamentation of sorrow. Their wish was only to say what they hoped had never been said before.

This seems quite unfair when we remember Donne's great love-poems or Marvell's *Definition of Love*; but we do not know how much Johnson had actually read. Notice that originality of idea had little attraction for the eighteenth-century critic; Pope had defined good writing as:

> What oft was thought, but ne'er so well expressed

—and all the art of the time seems to concentrate on the organisation of the known and civilised world. In this setting Donne's explorations of thought, image and verse-rhythm, or Herbert's and Vaughan's unworldly devotions, would have little appeal.

But Johnson's sensitivity and fairness could not allow him to condemn the Metaphysicals without some qualification:

> ... if they frequently threw away their wit upon false conceits, they likewise sometimes struck out unexpected truth: if their conceits were far-fetched, they were often worth the carriage. To write on their plan it was at least necessary to read and think.

It is not the praise we would give today, but in its time this was something of a defence of the poets.

ROMANTIC

The late eighteenth century was probably the time at which the reputation of the Metaphysicals was lowest, and very few people would know them. There is nothing, either, to suggest that any Romantic poet except Coleridge knew the Metaphysicals well, in spite of certain resemblances between Marvell and Keats, and Vaughan and Wordsworth, pointed out in the last chapter.

Hazlitt's *Lectures on the English Poets* (1818) may be worth quoting to reveal how little a critic lecturing on such a comprehensive subject was obliged to know about the Metaphysicals:

Of Donne I know nothing but some beautiful verses to his wife, dissuading her from accompanying him on his travels abroad, and some quaint riddles in verse, which the Sphinx could not unravel.

Coleridge is one of the greatest English critics, and in his *Lectures* (also of 1818), it is clear that he had read Donne, at least, with great appreciation. Many of Coleridge's comments are as directly relevant today as then, and he is one of the most helpful guides to the strength of Donne. The following extracts are worth considering carefully:

> To read Dryden, Pope, etc., you need only count syllables; but to read Donne you must measure *time,* and discover the time of each word by the sense of passion.
>
> After all, there is but one Donne! and now tell me yet, wherein, in *his own kind*, he differs from the similar power in Shakespeare?

In poets from Donne to Cowley, Coleridge says, 'we find the most fantastic out-of-the-way thoughts, but in the most pure and genuine mother English . . .'

Lastly, a particularly valuable bit of implied advice, from his comments on Donne's *The Canonization*:

> One of my favourite poems. As late as ten years ago, I used to seek and find out grand lines and fine stanzas; but my delight has been far greater since it has consisted more in tracing the leading thought thro'out the whole. The former is too much like coveting your neighbour's goods; in the latter you merge yourself in the author, you *become He*!

VICTORIAN

In the mid-nineteenth century, isolated readers noticed and liked the Metaphysicals. Swinburne said how much he preferred Donne to Gray; Gerard Manley Hopkins spoke of Herbert as his strongest tie to the English church, and of Marvell as 'a most rich and nervous poet'; and there are several places in Hopkins's poetry where he seems to borrow from the Metaphysicals: for example, the phrase 'air of angels' in *Henry Purcell*, the 'ah my dear' of *The Windhover* (compare Herbert's *Love*) and—seeming to echo Crashaw—several of the more elaborate and sensuous stanzas of *The Wreck of the Deutschland*. Robert Browning wrote frequently of Donne in his letters, with much appreciation. By the eighteen-nineties, several leading critics of the time—Saintsbury, Gosse, Raleigh and Dowden—wrote in praise of Donne, and the way was being quietly opened for the extraordinary revolution in taste which has taken place this century.

EARLY TWENTIETH CENTURY

Though some Victorians admired the Metaphysicals, there was often behind their praise the assumption that these were quaint and minor poets. Victorian preference was for the Romantics, and cleverness in poetry was still regarded as something of a mistake. Donne and the other great Metaphysical poets could not come fully into their own until critical tastes changed sharply; and this we find happening in the years preceding the First World War.

To one man must go much of the credit for the revival of the Metaphysicals—Herbert Grierson. In 1912, this scholar and critic produced an edition of *Donne's Poems* which is still very highly valued, both for its textual readings and its notes. Whether Grierson ever thought so highly of Donne as many of those to whom he introduced the poet is doubtful; in the 1912 edition he wrote—with a pejorative implication—that there was something of Tennyson in Donne (an idea most modern readers find it very hard to accept), and that Donne's mind was 'short of the highest gifts of serene imagination or serene wisdom'. But whatever Grierson's valuation of the poet, the 1912 *Donne* offered for a generation of young and searching readers the depth and strength they missed in much poetry of their time.

Rupert Brooke, a young Cambridge student who became himself a poet of startling popularity, made in his criticism several penetrating comments which show his appreciation of Donne. For example, Brooke wrote of 'that wider home which Donne knew better than any of the great English poets, the human heart.'

This is new praise for Donne: 'the human heart' was the kind

of term often used in relation to Romantic poetry, but—with
the exception of Shakespeare—seventeenth-century poets would
be praised for their relevance not to the heart but to the head;
that is, for their Wit, power, strength, subtlety and so on. But
Brooke repeats the observation elsewhere: 'It must not appear
that his humour, or his wit, or his passion alternated.' And
again: 'Donne could combine either the light or grave aspects
of love with this lack of solemnity that does but heighten the
sharpness of the seriousness.'

Another modern poet, W. B. Yeats, also discovered Donne in
Grierson's edition; and with Yeats the discovery was of immense
value for his own experience. Donne was, in a sense, confirming
for Yeats possibilities of lyric poetry which he had always sub-
consciously suspected; and in the bite and fervent dramatisation
of Yeats's later love-poetry there is much to suggest the influence
of the *Songs and Sonets*. Yeats wrote to Grierson:

> I notice that the more precise and learned the thought the greater
> the beauty, the passion; the intricacies and subtleties of his
> imagination are the length and depths of the furrow made by
> his passion. His pedantry and obscurity—the rock and loam of
> his Eden—but made me the more certain that one who is but a
> man like us all has seen God.

Another comment of Yeats is important:

> Donne could be as metaphysical as he pleased and yet never
> seemed inhuman and hysterical as Shelley often does because he
> could be as physical as he pleased.

LATER TWENTIETH CENTURY

These remarks of Brooke and Yeats are partial anticipation of
T. S. Eliot's better-known praise. Eliot's essay *The Metaphysical
Poets* was a review of a fine anthology by Herbert Grierson,
Metaphysical Lyrics and Poems of the Seventeenth Century, which
appeared in 1921. The Grierson Preface should be read as well
as the Eliot review. Eliot's essay explores more carefully, if
sometimes rather pompously ('a degree of heterogeneity of
material compelled into unity by the operation of the poet's

mind is omnipresent in poetry'), the ideas expressed rather vaguely by Brooke and colloquially by Yeats.

Brooke praises Donne for his knowledge of the heart, for his seriousness without solemnity, where 'the light or grave' aspects were combined, and for the way in which his humour, his wit and his passion worked *together at once*, not separately. Yeats notes how Donne's intellectual strength goes *with* his passion, not apart from it; 'his pedantry and his obscurity' somehow testify to his inspiration.

Eliot writes:

> The poets of the seventeenth century . . . possessed a mechanism of sensibility which could devour any kind of experience . . . In the seventeenth century a dissociation of sensibility set in, from which we have never recovered; and this dissociation, as is natural, was aggravated by the influence of the two most powerful poets of the century, Milton and Dryden.

Milton and Dryden were, Eliot suggests, specialists, where Donne, Shakespeare, Herbert and others had been poets who combined many different poetic abilities. Milton and Dryden are not under discussion in this book, but it has several times been said here how finely balanced are gaiety and seriousness, brilliance and simplicity, brainwork and emotion, in the Metaphysical poets. And most twentieth-century readers have felt that Eliot is right—that this balance is lacking in most eighteenth- or nineteenth-century poetry, which is excessive in one direction or another.

Since 1921, there has been an immense revival of the Metaphysicals. Their greatness is now generally acknowledged, and many critics have written on them at length—too many to be listed here. The books particularly recommended for readers of this book are listed in the bibliography which follows. Several of the best—Joan Bennett, F. R. Leavis, and Eliot himself, for example—are limited by the very fact that when they wrote they were young critics making a case for unpopular writers against a sceptical academic 'Establishment'. Their words have a ring, sometimes, of pleading, and sometimes they seem excited by discoveries which are not discoveries to a later age. But they are of great value to the reader who is himself only just discovering —more valuable by far than the learned American (or English) theses which assume an immensely detailed knowledge in their readers.

A SUMMING-UP

The story told in this chapter is a very brief guide to the tastes of English readers in different centuries, and to develop this historical sense adds greatly to one's appreciation of literature.

In Donne's own time his poetry was much admired for its originality, ingenuity and violent force. In Samuel Johnson's age these qualities were not admired so much as moderation, proportion, lucidity and a civilised restraint of feeling: Donne and his followers were more or less dismissed. In the nineteenth century they were little known, except to a few widely-read men, mostly poets themselves; poetry was considered to be mainly 'heart' ('passion') or 'soul', not 'head'. It was the period at which Wit was least valued.

The twentieth-century turn-about was closely linked to the reaction against Victorian attitudes which made itself felt in many spheres. Many people, anxious to be fashionable, were content to regard Donne as an 'in' writer; such preferences are of no importance. But there really was something in the Metaphysicals to appeal particularly to modern readers: an intellectual tautness, with repeatedly startling effects, and also the cheerful directness about love, which contrasted markedly with Victorian prudery. Again, it was Donne who was the main figure; perhaps for the first time his roughness and his insecurity came to seem qualities of distinction. Pessimism, religious doubt, the vivid fear of death, were for the first time not peculiar to Donne or 'melancholic' men, but to a great number; and a new search for intricacy in poetry and psychology discovered the Metaphysicals and gave them a closer and more careful attention than they had ever had before. We now think our present-day valuation to be correct; but it is a strange fact of English literary history that these poets should have had to wait so long for justice.

Bibliography

This has been kept deliberately brief, and suggests only a core of essential reading. Many more books and hundreds of articles have, of course, been written.

ANTHOLOGIES

H. J. C. Grierson, ed.: *Metaphysical Lyrics and Poems* (Oxford, 1921).
Helen Gardner, ed.: *The Metaphysical Poets* (Penguin).
Fred Inglis, ed.: *English Poetry 1550–1660* (Methuen).
H. J. Massingham, ed.: *Treasury of Seventeenth Century English Verse* (Macmillan, 1919).

TEXTS

Donne

H. J. C. Grierson, ed.: *Poems,* 2 vols. (Oxford, 1912).
John Hayward, ed.: *Complete Poems and Selected Prose* (Nonesuch Press, 1929).
Helen Gardner, ed.: *Divine Poems* (Oxford, 1952).
Theodore Redpath, ed.: *Songs and Sonets* (Methuen, 1956).
John Hayward, ed.: *Selected Poems* (Penguin, 1950).

Herbert

A. Waugh, ed.: *Poems* (World's Classics, Oxford, 1907). *Temple and the Priest to the Temple* (Everyman, Dent).
F. E. Hutchinson, ed.: *Works* (Oxford, 1941).
Douglas Brown, ed.: *Selected Poems* (Hutchinson, 1960).

Crashaw

L. C. Martin, ed.: *Poems,* 2nd ed. (Oxford, 1927).

Marvell

H. M. Margoliouth, ed.: *Poems and Letters* (Oxford, 1927).

Vaughan

L. C. Martin, ed.: *Works* (Oxford, 1914).

CRITICISM

(a) General

The *Prefaces* to the anthologies listed above are most helpful.

Joan Bennett: *Four Metaphysical Poets* (Cambridge, 1934).

T. S. Eliot: 'The Metaphysical Poets' in *Selected Essays* (Faber, 1932).

Boris Ford, ed.: *From Donne to Marvell* (Vol. 3 of *Pelican Guide to English Literature*, Penguin, 1956).

Samuel Johnson: 'Life of Cowley' in *Lives of the Poets* (1779).

F. R. Leavis: 'The Line of Wit' in *Revaluation* (Chatto & Windus, 1936).

James Smith: 'On Metaphysical Poetry' in *Scrutiny*, and *Determinations*, ed. F. R. Leavis (Chatto & Windus, 1934).

(b) Particular Poets

J. B. Leishman: *The Monarch of Wit* [Donne] (Hutchinson .1951).

T. S. Eliot: *George Herbert* (British Council: Longmans, 1962).

L. C. Knights: 'George Herbert' in *Explorations* (Chatto & Windus, 1946).

J. H. Summers: *George Herbert: His Religion and Art* (Chatto & Windus, 1954).

F. E. Hutchinson: *Henry Vaughan* (Oxford, 1947).

T. S. Eliot: 'Andrew Marvell' in *Selected Essays* (Faber, 1932).

Index

The page-numbers listed are those on which part or all of a poem is discussed or analysed. Casual references or mere quotations are not indexed here.